W9-AHT-202

i

HEALING IMAGES FOR CHILDREN

Teaching Relaxation and Guided Imagery to Children Facing Cancer and Other Serious Illnesses

BY NANCY C. KLEIN

ILLUSTRATED BY MATTHEW HOLDEN

Published by

INNER COACHING

Watertown, Wisconsin

Publisher's Cataloging-in-Publication
(Provided by Quality Books, Inc.)

Klein, Nancy C.
      Healing images for children : teaching relaxation and guided imagery to children
   facing cancer and other serious illnesses / by Nancy C. Klein ; illustrated
   by Matthew Holden. -- 1st ed.
      p. cm.
      Includes bibliographical references and index.
      LCCN 00-135936
      ISBN 0-9636027-2-1

      1. Children--Diseases--Therapy. 2. Imagery
   (Psychology)--Therapeutic use. 3. Tumors in children.
   I. Holden, Matthew. II. Title.

      RC489.F35K54 2000   615.8'51
                                     QBI00-901694

Family Circus, copyright 10/12/99, reprinted with special permission King Features Syndicate.
The stories "Dream On" and "Pleasant Dreams" by Jeffrey S. Allen, copyright 1996, reprinted
by permission of author.
The poem "Hope" by Mary Soergel, reprinted by permission of author.

Illustrated by Matthew Holden
Cover & book interior design by Joel Richter
Cover illustration by Lori Grabske
Edited by Staci Leigh O'Brien

Published by Inner Coaching
1108 Western Avenue
Watertown, Wisconsin 53094
(920) 262-0439

The material in this book is provided for educational and informational purposes only, and is
not intended to be a substitute for medical advice. A physician or appropriate health care professional should always be consulted for any health or medical condition. The author and publisher
disclaim any liability or loss, personal or otherwise, resulting from the use by readers of the
methods set forth in this book.

Printed in the United States of America on acid-free paper

First Edition

DEDICATION

This book is dedicated to:

my parents, Carol and Gerald G. Schmidt, who rooted me in my faith and steadfastly demonstrate faith in action.

my daughter Kendra Christine Klein, who opened her soul and shared gifts of spirit and wisdom to guide me.

my son, Bradley David Klein, who shared his sense of humor and creativity with me and never wavered in his belief in the project.

my husband, Roger Klein, who each day, through his love, instills confidence that I can meet the challenges ahead of me.

Their honesty, support, and encouragement enabled me to continually reach toward the highest goals for this book.

TABLE OF CONTENTS

PART 1
Information for Parents, Health Care Team Members, and Other Caregivers

PART 2
Information and Stories to Share with Children

An easy way to locate this section is to look for the stars on each page.

RESOURCES

ACKNOWLEDGEMENTS

This book would not have been possible without the cooperation and assistance of the following staff members at the University of Wisconsin Children's Hospital, Department of Pediatric Hematology/Oncology Clinic:

My deepest thanks to Joel Wish, Ph.D., Director of Health Psychology, Pediatric Team Leader, Clinical Associate Professor-Departments of Rehabilitation Medicine and Pediatrics, for his limitless enthusiasm and support from the very first day that I articulated my goals and through each phase of research and writing. It was his belief in the project that gave me the confidence to go forward.

To Sharon Frierdich, Nurse Practitioner; Jan Lehmann, Nurse Clinician; Denise Anacker, Nurse/Care Team Leader; Marianne Tripp, Hospital School Nurse; and Stephanie Farrell, Post Doctoral Fellow in Pediatric Health Psychology, all of whom reviewed the manuscript for medical accuracy and offered their expertise gained from their daily work with the families for whom this work is intended.

In addition, I wish to thank the following people:

Andrew Pojman, Psy.D., Clinical Psychologist, who understood my hopes for the book and helped me focus its broad scope with incredible clarity. His insights and encouragement were essential for the development of the sections for adults.

Linda Picchi, M.A., who offered support as a friend and her expertise as a reading specialist to the content of the sections for children.

Oncology nurses Marni Fisher and Sue Westring, for support and assistance with medical content. Their professional experiences helped identify authentic concerns of families and children facing illness.

Mary Soergel and Al Wilson, Ph.D., caring counselors and co-founders of Stillwaters Center, Inc., whose daily support of people living with cancer give them insights into the feelings people bring to serious illness and the healing that can occur with any prognosis. Mary and Al not only helped my writing, but also helped me on my own healing journey.

Reverend Jack Hicks, gifted in the ministry of the spirit, who enriched the book and my life with his wisdom and his deep understanding of people.

My friends — Karen Kwapil, Vicki Allen, Linda Franken, Sara Clark, and Carol Engel who read my first drafts and urged me to follow my heart.

Jeff Allen, M.Ed., for encouragement, project coordination, and creative vision. Jeff contributed the active imagination stories "Pleasant Dreams" and "Dream On."

Staci Leigh O'Brien, editor and friend, for exquisite consideration of each word and each message throughout the book.

Joel Richter for his artistry and creativity. Joel took a manuscript and transformed it into an inviting book.

Lori Grabske for the beautiful cover artwork. I was truly inspired by her talent and her loving offer to interpret my healing image.

My deepest love and thanks to my children: Kendra Klein, who read each word many times with such care that she was able to "listen" to the messages and feel their authenticity, and Brad Klein, who captured a child's sense of fantasy and enriched the stories with vivid details.

And to my husband, Roger Klein, Psy.D., Clinical Psychologist, whose research into the effectiveness of imagery and relaxation strategies for children provided the foundation for this book.

FOREWORD

A diagnosis of cancer, or other serious illness, poses tremendous stress on both patient and family. When the patient is a child, it is in many respects even more difficult, especially for parents and family members. There has been increasing attention paid to the emotional impact from such illnesses, but there has been far less attention given to what to do about it and specifically, how to provide support for children with serious illnesses.

This guide provides excellent insights into daily problems and suggests specific strategies and ideas about how to cope. It also provides constructive, helpful support. There is an increasing world-wide interest in the mind-body connection and we have entered an era where increasing emphasis is given to positive thinking, mental imagery, relaxation, and other strategies to help cope with difficult situations. The possibility that such activities may even improve treatment outcomes is exciting and hopeful. At the very least, such efforts improve the quality of life during difficult times.

This powerful book is written for patients and their families. The author has drawn on her own insights and experiences as a teacher, parent, and patient and has created a wonderful guide that will help both children and adults. It is to be read and re-read through the journey of serious illness.

— Richard M. Hansen, MD
   President
   Stillwaters Center, Inc.
   Cancer Support Services

INTRODUCTION

Healing Images for Children is a book for families and professionals who are helping children cope with serious childhood illnesses. It offers support for parents who seek an active role in their child's treatment program. It provides children with tools to combat stress. The emphasis is on helping children develop a coping response to their illness and the medical procedures used to treat their illness. It may be comfortably used in a home or medical setting. The title, *Healing Images,* suggests that when facing challenges, we can hold pictures, images, in our minds and hearts that help us focus on feelings that bring us strength and a belief in healing.

The book is actually written for two audiences: children facing illness and those who care for them. It is a book to be shared between adults and children. This is appropriate because the experience of a child's illness is one that is shared between the child and those who love and care for the child. Parents, as well as others involved with the care of an ill child, will find helpful strategies within this book, however, it is not written as a how-to manual. Each family's needs and experiences are different, yet there are things to be shared along the way. It serves as a guide to point out important landmarks on a journey.

The first section is aimed at adults. It describes effective research-based relaxation techniques. The techniques work because they are based in the knowledge that feelings of stress and feelings of relaxation cause physical changes in our bodies. This is often referred to as the mind-body connection. The second part is written for children. The information sections introduce medical terms and experiences. The stories describe relaxation techniques as well as convey messages of strength and hope.

Goals of this Book

- **To give children concrete information that will help guide them through their treatments.**

  Descriptions of many medical interventions that will become part of the child's world are written at a child's comprehension level. New and possibly confusing terms are explained and incorporated into a context a child can understand.

- **To provide children with stories that encourage the use of relaxation and active imagination to reduce the pain and anxiety that may accompany their illness.**

  The stories reframe the medical and emotional aspects of the illness with positive statements that reinforce hope and a sense of confidence in one's ability to cope with difficulties.

- **To offer an overview of studies that demonstrate the effectiveness of relaxation and imagery when dealing with stressful situations.**

  Parents and other caregivers will receive background information on mind-body visualizations and the field of psychoneuroimmunology. References to supportive research are provided for those who would like to do additional reading.

You do not need to read the book cover-to-cover in order to begin using it. Go directly to the sections you need, as you need them. Come back to the other parts when you are able. Chapter 8, *"Getting Started"* offers a brief overview of many of the important aspects of the book. It may be a helpful place to begin as well as to review at the end.

Read the children's section on your own to preview the stories and then read it with your child. Your child may have the reading skills to work through it independently, but as you share it, you will have many opportunities to clear up confusions your child may have and offer support and encouragement as new experiences are presented.

The book is separated by a title page indicating where the section to share with children begins. This section is easy to locate because the pages have stars on them. The illustrations accompanying the active imagination stories are designed to be open-ended and lead you to your own visual symbols. They were drawn to be gender and age neutral so that each child could use them as a beginning point to create a personal picture in his or her own mind's eye.

There are places within the children's pages to add personal entries. I encourage you to color the pictures, write on the pages, and adapt the stories in any way. This book is for your individual journey.

A Healing Images for Children CD is available from Inner Coaching. It consists of progressive muscle relaxation exercises and several active imagination stories from the book. It is offered to give your child ready access to important methods for coping with stress and discomfort. Listening to the CD also provides a model and guide for reading aloud the stories within the book. The last track on the CD is a musical selection that can be used in several ways. It can be played to set a relaxing mood or it can be used as background music if the reader would like to record personal tapes.

About the Artwork and the Artist

The artist, Matt Holden, is a college student majoring in art. Matt is a cancer survivor. He was treated for cancer when he was 12 years old. He provided the following comments about himself and his art.

"When I was being treated for Lymphoma, a book called *St. George and the Dragon* was given to me. It is about a hero's long and difficult battle with an evil dragon. I read it many times and it became very special to me. The symbolism was obvious and simple, but the romantic story and beautiful artwork of the book influenced me greatly. It was a real and visual representation of my condition: I was St. George and I was fighting a cruel and oftentimes overwhelmingly powerful monster. Four and a half years later, I chose St. George to be my Confirmation name.

Art has always been an enormous part of my life. The premises of St. George and the Dragon have inspired me not only emotionally and spiritually, but artistically as well. I base a lot of my artwork on the conflict between two forces — many times good versus evil. I've created countless pictures of men fighting monsters. Not only does it make a cool picture, but also it is representative of a part of my life. I love art because it is such a wonderful means of self-expression. I believe expressing yourself is an extremely important part of living and dealing with conflict.

The art in this book is intended to be a real and visual representation of the fighting, healing, and self-expression that is, in a way, part of every person living with cancer. However, each drawing is to be open and interpretive. It is very important that the reader does not see the artist's image created from the stories, but sees his or her own. The figures in the pictures are of no particular race or gender. They are exactly what the reader sees them as. The illustrations were designed to be visual aides in establishing actual healing devices the reader will create in his or her own mind and body."

Chapter 1

HEADING INTO ROCKY WATERS – A DIAGNOSIS

With a diagnosis of a life-threatening illness, you enter a new world overnight. The future is unknown and family routines are disrupted, often for extended periods. There is no turning back. Questions and confusions turn the arrow on the compass so fast that at first it seems difficult to get your bearings and move in the right direction. You must travel a challenging new path.

It is one thing to face a personal illness, but to face a child's crisis is of another magnitude. Parents feel their own fears as well as their child's. Despite the turbulence in their own hearts, parents must be calm, strong, and compassionate with their child.

There are days, sometimes weeks, of dealing with suspicions that something might be wrong. There are visits to doctors and numerous tests before a diagnosis can be confirmed with hope, denial, and fear at each event. When the diagnosis is

2

made and parents know what they are facing, they must choose a path, a direction. They must put one foot before the other and move ahead.

A new journey is beginning. We do not know the twists and turns ahead of us, but it is still a journey. We should consider the things we normally do before we begin a trip. On other trips that we take in life, we prepare as much as we can ahead of time. We check maps. We pack appropriate clothes and equipment. We ask neighbors to watch over our house while we are away. We check with others who have already made the trip and we ask for recommendations about what things to be sure to do and what things to avoid. We buy a guidebook and research the events and places ahead of us on our travels.

This book is a resource for the journey ahead. It is a guide to help you find a direction that weaves body, mind, and spirit into the healing journey.

LIGHTHOUSES ~ A HEALING IMAGE

A trip to the ocean is frequently a travel destination for me. I find it rejuvenates and relaxes me. Over the past several years I developed a fascination with lighthouses and searched for them on my vacations. At first, I thought that my interest in lighthouses stemmed only from my vacation visits. Now, I believe there was a larger meaning.

A lighthouse has several functions. One is to illuminate the dark waters. After an eighteen-year remission from cancer, a recurrence of the life-threatening illness plunged me into dark waters. The symbol of a lighthouse began to become clear to me during the challenging days following the diagnosis. In my quiet moments, I frequently found myself visualizing the bright beam of a lighthouse to guide me in my healing. I pictured a beacon of light pouring into me and scanning my body searching for cancer cells for my immune system to destroy. I pictured God's healing light filling me.

It was a surprise when prior to beginning radiation treatments, I received a National Cancer Institute booklet from the hospital with a picture of a lighthouse on its cover. The beam of light was symbolic of the power of the radiation treatments I was about to begin. My visualizations now had a second meaning for me—God's healing light—medicine's healing light. It was obvious to me that I had found a meaningful symbol, a healing image, for my journey to recovery. I began to put pictures of lighthouses around my home to help me focus on healing. I used these visual images of light and lighthouses daily during my quiet times and during my treatments.

Guided by the Light

A lighthouse has another function beyond lighting the waters. It also serves as a guide, as a sentinel on watch to warn of danger and to alert sailors to change course to a safer route. This is a symbol for a parent with a child who is facing a life-threatening illness. For the captain of a ship, the rocks ahead may seem ominous and overpowering, but the ever-vigilant lighthouse keeper uses light and sound to steer ships away from danger.

Parents can have equally effective ways of guiding children who are thrust into the dark, rocky waters of a serious illness. Parents know there are dangerous waters ahead for their child, and they can become steady beacons that will lead away from the rocks to calmer waters.

This book offers beacons to light the way for families on a journey of healing.

CHARTING A NEW COURSE

My own journey began twenty years ago with a diagnosis of breast cancer. I was 29 years old and the mother of two preschool-aged children. With the diagnosis, my life changed. I entered a time of turmoil and transition. I was stunned by how quickly I needed to learn to live in a world with no guarantees. It was necessary for me to chart a new course through life.

When I was first diagnosed, I had to make major decisions within a very short period of time. I realized that the decisions I made would affect me emotionally and physically, and possibly impact the future length of my life. I was unprepared, but staying that way was not an option for me. I wanted to participate in the decisions, or at the very least, feel comfortable with my understanding of the decisions being made. I faced a mountain of information about cancer and its treatments. I didn't have background experiences to help me integrate the large volume of medical information available. I needed help.

I reached out for resources that offered healing therapies. I read books that provided inspiration and information. I searched for strength through my faith, the steadiness and love of my family, and the outpouring of support from friends. I sought out others whose lives had been interrupted by cancer. I also reached inward.

The turtle became a symbol for me. I seemed to tuck my head inside my shell and spend time exploring my heart and soul. Images came to me that strengthened me and provided a sense of peace and comfort. I used those images in my fight against cancer. I was also able to use prayer to talk with God and listen for God's presence.

Like a rock hitting the surface of a calm lake, sending out waves of disturbance, the diagnosis rocked the lives of those close to me. My fear was that I would not be there for my children or my husband in the future. Yet, week by week, then month by month, and finally, with each passing year of continuing good health, I let cancer recede from the forefront of my life. I took a deep breath, believed I would be around for awhile, and planned for the future. I became involved in my family's expanding activities and I returned to teaching.

When my eighteen-year remission ended with a recurrence of cancer, I felt like the pieces of my life had been tossed into the air and tumbled into a heap. All the professional tasks, family responsibilities, and social activities I thought were so important came to a screeching halt as I searched again for meaning. Now what? I mourned the many non-death losses associated with cancer as I faced the uncertainty of my future with stage IV metastatic cancer.

Yet, through my days of sadness and my winter of listening, I found anchors for my faith. Each treatment and each dose of medication became an opportunity to pray and use healing visualizations. I fully embraced hope. Once again, I put together a foundation for coping with illness.

Cancer seemed nondescript to me. What was it that was consuming me? Creating visual symbols helped me focus on "concrete" healing images rather than the vague idea of cancer cells inside my body. The visualizations gave me a way to talk to myself with positive messages about healing and to quiet the fears that spun in my head. During each treatment and throughout each day, I continued to develop "pictures" in my mind that gave me strength, peace, and a belief in healing.

Guiding a Child

As I went through my own cancer treatments, I found myself thinking of children facing serious illnesses. I wondered what the experiences were like for a child. I have worked for twenty-five years as a teacher of children with special needs, and it was natural for me to think of how I could help and teach a child. In fact, I couldn't avoid it. In my mind, I am always "teaching" children. I thought of how I would explain illness, diagnostic tests, and treatments to a child. I knew how I had found strength and peace and I knew children and their families would benefit from similar strategies.

For centuries, stories have been used to help people learn to cope with life's problems. Likewise, even before Aesop, teachers used short stories to help children understand a confusing world. For many years teachers have taught children and their parents how to use one's imagination as a way of helping children master essential skills (DeMille 1976). In recent times, short stories have been created to help children understand specific medical procedures and to teach children specific skills that will help them heal after the procedure is completed (Crowe 1999).

I know that children learn when they are able to make pictures in their minds. They are storytellers and operate easily in a world rich with fantasy. They learn best when they can associate new information to previous experiences, which enables them to create meaningful connections. Children, as well as adults, build upon what they know. Yet, few of us have the background experiences that equip us to deal with the rapid decisions and adjustments that must be made at the time of a medical crisis. We need resources.

A Starting Point

How can we help a child gain a sense of strength and control over a disease with treatment protocols that are frightening and go against the natural impulses of a child? Treatment requires times of uncustomary stillness for children who would rather be running outside. How can we help a child lie still on a treatment table?

Each of the many appointments, tests, and treatments require bravery. How can we bolster a child's sense of courage and safety? Is it possible to avoid fear spilling from one painful experience to all aspects of therapy? Is it possible to encourage a child to use language to express his or her needs amidst all the new terminology? How best to anticipate frightening confusions about words being used in a medical context which have very different meanings in the child's world?

Recuperation creates times of isolation and inactivity. How can we help a child connect to friends and find stimulating activities? Can sadness and depression be alleviated or averted? How does a child interpret a serious illness?

There are no simple answers to such complex questions, but it is my belief that within each child, strengths and coping strategies can be nurtured. With these questions in mind, I began writing stories that provide tools for a child to use to gain a sense of courage, of peace, and of confidence when facing the difficulties of treatment for cancer and other serious illnesses. The stories use analogies from background experiences common to most children. Using these stories as examples, a child will find a starting point for creating his or her personalized healing images.

The stories are opportunities for a child and adult to share gentle, positive experiences. They provide a balance to the medical experiences the family is going through that are difficult and that are a struggle. With each story, an adult coaches the child through an exercise that teaches the child how to achieve muscle relaxation. Next, a story theme is introduced with imagery that addresses an aspect of diagnosis, treatment, side effects, or emotional responses. Within each story, the child is asked to repeat a positive phrase to reinforce and anchor the healing image. We all need help finding words to describe our feelings when faced with a life-threatening illness and the stories that follow provide a common language between parent and child.

Key Elements

As parents and caregivers learn about the use of relaxation, active imagination, and positive statements, they are able to coach their child in the use of these strategies and help their child and themselves cope with the experiences surrounding an illness. These elements help a family lay a foundation for ways to support one's immune system and to cope with stressful situations:

- *Progressive muscle relaxation* provides a tool to calm the body and mind.
- *Active imagination* trains a child to refocus attention away from discomfort and fear to images that are pleasant and comforting.
- *Positive statements* provide a basis for self-talk, the things we say to ourselves, that reinforce our movement toward achieving goals.

The quiet moments spent with the stories will strengthen the bond between the adult and child and their sense of working as a team. The stories provide caregivers with concrete tools they can employ to help their child create feelings of calmness. Working with the stories offers opportunities to take an active role in a medical environment that often requires dependency and a need for the acceptance that others will be caring for us.

In sharing these stories, parents and caregivers will be buoyed on rough seas knowing they are offering tangible life rafts to their child. They will have the joy of seeing their strength reflected back to them as their child manages the journey through dark waters with courage beyond expectations.

The story below has long held meaning for me as a teacher. It also reflects my hope for this collection of stories.

The Young Boy and the Starfish

An elderly man was taking a sunrise walk along the beach the morning following a storm. The beach was littered with thousands of starfish that had been tossed ashore in the storm's violent waves.

In the distance the man caught sight of a young boy who seemed to be dancing along the waves. As he got closer he saw that the boy was picking up starfish from the sand and gently tossing them back into the ocean.

"What are you doing?" the man asked the boy.

"The sun is coming up, and the tide is going out. If I throw them back into the water they will live," replied the boy.

"But, young man, there are miles of beach with starfish all along. How can you make any difference?"

The young boy bent down, picked up another small starfish and threw it lovingly back into the ocean past the breaking waves.

"I made a difference for that one," he replied.

— Author Unknown

The children's stories that follow are gifts to be picked up as shells along the beach. Some of the shells will seem more beautiful, more special than others. Some shells will become treasures. They are written for you and for the special, precious child in your life. I hope you will find treasures on your walk.

Chapter 2

CONNECTING THE MIND AND BODY

Here's something interesting to think about: psychoneuroimmunology. Quite a mouthful to say, yet still easier than the childhood favorite supercalifragilisticexpialidocious. Mary Poppins, the famous nanny from the children's story, was onto something when she sang, "a spoonful of sugar helps the medicine go down." Mary knew that we feel better about something unpleasant when we pair it with something that we like. A positive attitude helps us do difficult tasks. Researchers have gone far beyond Mary in understanding this mind-body connection.

Psychoneuroimmunology (PNI) is a science that examines the physical reactions that occur in our bodies and minds. It means that psyche, the mind and all of its functions (thoughts, beliefs, attitudes, planning, and imagination), is related to neuro, the nervous system, which is essentially the chemical system of the body (Simonton & Henson 1992).

Dr. Joan Borysenko, co-founder of the Mind-Body clinic at Beth Israel Hospital in Boston, discusses the scientific evidence of a direct link between the brain, the mind, the emotions, and the immune system in her book, *Minding the Body, Mending the Mind*. The links are chemical messengers called neuropeptides that are transmitted through body fluids. These molecules are produced in the brain when you have a thought or an emotion.

The immune system does not operate independently from the rest of the body or mind. If you are experiencing stress and feel anxious or worried, chemicals such as epinephrine, norepinephrine, and cortisol are produced and then received by cells all over the body. When the cells in the immune system receive these chemicals, immune function may be suppressed. However, optimistic emotions produce favorable chemicals such as interferons and interleukins. When cells in the immune system receive these chemicals, the immune system is strengthened (Achterberg 1985).

Responses to Stress

Research clearly shows that our bodies respond to stress. During stressful experiences, adrenaline and hormones are released, and the nervous system is activated, sharpening our senses. Simultaneously, our pulse rises, our respiration rate increases, and our muscles tense to ready us to react to the emergency. This is called the "fight or flight" response, and it's great for emergencies that require physical action. When you are threatened, it gets your body ready to flee or to fight because you sense impending danger (Benson 1975).

Yet in modern times, these same autonomic (involuntary) physiological responses occur regardless of the stressful conditions — most of which are emotional rather than physical. Our bodies create the physical changes but we do not act on them. These responses can create a state of "exhaustion" if there is continuous exposure to the same or similar stressors. These stress responses negatively impact our immune system and make us more vulnerable to illness (Simon 1999).

Consider these implications when facing your child's illness. A life-threatening illness becomes a major source of stress and many emotional and physical reactions are activated. These feelings are registered in our bodies at the cellular level and can have a detrimental effect on our immune system, so it is important that we help ourselves, as well as our children, acquire skills to counteract the negative impacts of stress.

The ability to turn off, or turn down, stress responses has also been widely researched. Herbert Benson, associate professor of medicine at Harvard Medical School, describes a technique in his book, *The Relaxation Response*, which can be used to quiet the aroused nervous system. Benson describes the Relaxation Response as a natural, innate mechanism that helps a person diminish the harmful bodily effects of stress and brings one's body back into a healthier balance.

To activate the Relaxation Response one can incorporate a quiet environment, a comfortable position, a receptive attitude, and the use of a repeated word or phrase. Benson states that using the technique for ten or twenty minutes once or twice daily may have a profound influence on one's ability to deal with difficult situations. Dr. Benson recognizes that these components are also found in meditation practices as well as in religious prayers (Gorfinkle 1998).

The stories in the children's section can also help access the Relaxation Response. Using the active imagination stories is one step on the path to helping your child redirect his or her thinking to ways that increase strength and diminish stress responses. The exercises cue the child to slow down his or her breathing and become calm and relaxed. The stories provide children with the tools to:

- Think about medical events in a context that helps them make sense of what is happening to them. From this, they gain the understanding that there is a meaning and a reason for their treatments and other components of their illness.
- Use language to describe what they are feeling, allowing them to approach new circumstances with less stress. By naming these feelings, uncertainty

is diminished and confidence is increased. Confidence in one's ability to succeed leads to an optimistic outlook.

- Activate their imaginations in ways that may help them find solutions to some of the problems associated with illness. For example, if your child has learned to use a relaxation strategy or distraction technique when a blood test is being taken, your child will approach the event with a feeling of confidence about his or her ability to cope with discomfort. Stressful feelings will be diminished.

Coping in a Crisis

Children can be equipped to change their perception of their illness and treatments and face medical treatment with positive feelings. Even though we cannot remove the illness or stop the medical procedures, we know from the research on the mind-body connection, that our perceptions can have an influence on our physiological reactions.

With the understanding that feelings create physical responses, it is critical to understand that negative emotions are not to be feared. They are to be recognized as normal components in any crisis. There are intense feelings connected to hospitals, medical tests, and treatments, and it is appropriate to release these feelings. Our challenge is to embrace our child's full range of emotions and encourage their expression. It is not necessary to always have and express positive feelings. It is the repression of emotions, not their expression that contributes to increased stress levels.

Our emotions can be expressed in ways that help us feel better. As an example, on one occasion when my daughter was extremely angry, we took raw eggs and labeled them with the objects of her frustration. We found a safe place outside for her to throw the eggs, and as they smashed into the ground, the effect was so dramatic that we both ended up laughing. Expressing feelings in a positive way can lead to new meaning and renewed strength.

Although we do not always have control over the things that happen to us, or to those whom we love, we do have control over how we react. We have the choice of what to do with our experiences. This means we do not have to feel like a victim no matter what difficulties happen to us. Research demonstrates that this makes a difference to our well being and even makes changes in our bodies at the cellular level.

Rabbi Harold Kushner, author of *When Bad Things Happen To Good People*, and father of a terminally ill child, writes in his book:

Let me suggest that the bad things that happen to us in our lives do not have a meaning when they happen to us. They do not happen for any good reason, which could cause us to accept them willingly. But we can give them meaning. We can redeem these tragedies from senselessness by imposing meaning on them. The question we should be asking is not "Why did this happen to me? What did I do to deserve this?" This is really an unanswerable, pointless question. A better question would be, "Now that this has happened to me, what am I going to do about it?"

No one deserves to have a serious illness, or for their child to have to struggle with one, but the following chapters offer suggestions and steps you can take to answer the question, "Now what am I going to do about it?"

12

Chapter 3
BUILDING A PATH

Healthy images increase your sense of power, well-being, and peace of mind. They strengthen your sense of connectedness with your inner wisdom, with others, and with the world and the universe.
— O. Carl Simonton, *Healing Journey*

L
ike the garden stepping stones I see in specialty shops engraved with words such as Imagine, Dream, or Believe, we can build our own paths to healing with stepping stones that reflect our beliefs and our dreams. The stones that I choose for my path may not fit your footsteps and vice versa. We must each evaluate our attitudes toward life and use the strategies we are willing to believe in.

Spiritual beliefs, love, compassion, and hope are some of the ways we care for others and ourselves. Consider each of these, as well as the strategies offered in *Healing Images for Children*, as pieces of the path you are assembling. Think about where they fit in the picture of your life.

Ask yourself what your strengths are and what you need for balance in your life as you confront illness. Add pieces that enrich your life and take you toward peace of mind. Consider pieces that reflect your emotional, physical, psychological, and spiritual values.

As you build your path, your child will be building one, too. You will help by providing the resources, but it will be your child's personal path. Look for things that bring your child joy. Reassure your child. Listen to your child. Verbalize your love.

Most of us are motivated to learn coping strategies when we are confronted with a challenging situation. This has been true for me as well. Relaxation strategies have entered my life at different times and my use of them has evolved through the years. As I learned about the effects of progressive muscle relaxation, breathing, positive self-talk, imagery, music, and humor, they became part of my personal resources that I can draw upon when needed.

Children benefit from these same strategies, but it takes instruction and practice for them to see the way these techniques work together. It requires motivation. As an adult, my motivation was clear to me. Children need help. They need an adult to help them practice and to cue them when to use specific coping strategies.

In the following sections, an overview of techniques that counteract stress is provided with references to the research supporting their effectiveness. The same ideas are introduced to your child throughout the children's sections.

PROGRESSIVE MUSCLE RELAXATION

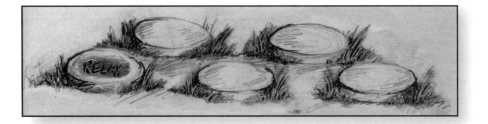

Progressive Muscle Relaxation (PMR) is a tool for learning body awareness and stress reduction. In progressive muscle relaxation you move through the body, tensing each muscle group, holding the tension, then releasing the tension.

Edmund Jacobson, an American physician, developed the approach in the 1940's. He proved that even when a person *imagined* tensing or moving a specific muscle its electrical energy changed (Borysenko 1987).

I first learned about progressive muscle relaxation when I was in high school. Our physical education teacher incorporated PMR into the curriculum. At the end of class we rested on the gym mats as the teacher guided us to relax our arms, hands, legs, and so on. It took several sessions before I learned to release the tension and feel the subtle changes between tight muscles and relaxed muscles. It is one of the most valuable, life-long skills I learned in high school. For years afterwards, whenever I used PMR, I always pictured myself in my gym suit!

A relaxation technique, like PMR, is used to help people reverse the negative physiological effects of stress. Research has concluded that the unconscious mind is more open to suggestion when people are relaxed, so using PMR with imagery allows a person to become more focused and receptive to the messages of stories.

All family members benefit from methods to reduce stress during the difficult days of dealing with life threatening illness and PMR can be used by all.

BREATHING

My understanding of the power of breathing came during Lamaze classes as I prepared for childbirth. For eight weeks we were instructed in breathing techniques that could increase relaxation and diminish discomfort. Our instructor insisted we practice at home and my motivation was very high to do so. I can clearly recall how after several weeks of practice, I finally had the "aha" moment of understanding how to work with my breathing. And thank goodness for the practice, because I was able to benefit from the techniques during labor and delivery. This type of breathing is used to help distract a person from pain and to help her stay in control.

Breathing also serves another purpose in stress reduction. Dr. David Simon, in his book *Return to Wholeness*, suggests focusing attention on a rhythmic pattern of breathing to interrupt the endless conversations that each of us hold within ourselves. It can help a person achieve a state of deep relaxation.

The active imagination stories in the children's chapter called *"Helping with Painful Sensations"* help a child with both types of breathing.

ACTIVE IMAGINATION AND POSITIVE SELF-STATEMENTS

After my diagnosis of cancer I read about the research by Drs. O. Carl Simonton and Stephanie Matthews-Simonton on using creative visualizations to enhance the body's immune system to strengthen its response against disease. A pioneer in the use of guided imagery for cancer patients, Dr. Simonton suggested using visualizations to enhance the function of the immune system, the healing part of the body. He coached patients to visualize cancer cells as aliens in a fight against an army of defending white blood cells (Simonton 1978). These concepts were new to me at the time, but I was very interested in the technique. I began to use visualizations to help me confront cancer.

A simple example of imagery that we are all familiar with is sitting around with friends talking about our experiences on a great vacation. As we talk to our friends, we are able to make mental snapshots and can relive the experience. The imagery is so real that we are able to see, hear, feel, and smell the memories from our trip.

People use guided imagery all the time. The use of imagery has been found by psychologists to be a powerful tool to help people change their perceptions. The use of imagery can help a child look at an experience in a new lens.

Imagine That...

Using active imagination stories is helpful because studies have discovered that chemical changes occur in our bodies not only in reaction to stress, but also in response to relaxation and imagery. Vividly imagining an event produces physiological effects nearly identical to actually experiencing the event itself. This effect is the reason that many athletes use imagery to increase their performance. The key concept of imagery in sports, and performances of any kind, is the belief that when people imagine themselves successfully performing a specific task, they increase their ability to achieve their goal.

Jeanne Achterberg states in her book *Imagery in Healing*:

[I]mages cause profound physiological change, a fact that must not be obscured by the glamour of modern medicine. Regardless of technological advancement, we will always have to contend with the vast complex of expectancies, beliefs, motivations, and the sometimes belligerent, sometimes miraculous, role of the imagination.

Visualizations can be created for a variety of purposes. A calming image can be used at night to settle down. An image of strength and energy can bolster a person who is feeling fatigued. When we use images of pleasant scenes we feel refreshed. Images of healing can be created to focus on any part of the body that requires care and restoration. Visualizations can also be used to block, or distract, thoughts.

Children will naturally have fantasies, some of which may be pleasant and calming, but others may be agitating or scary. The goal is to help your child focus on fantasies that are positive in order to override the negative notion of what it means to be ill. Your child can use the vivid, pleasant images in the active imagination stories to paint calming, enjoyable pictures in his or her mind. These images can be used to transform uncomfortable feelings into sensations that are more tolerable and less frightening.

Positive Self-Statements

An important component of active imagination stories are positive self-statements. Think for a moment about the thoughts racing through your head in regard to your child's illness. Some of your self-talk may include thoughts like, "I really trust our doctor," or "I'm not sure this new treatment is going to work," or "My boss does not understand the demands on me right now." You will find that your self-talk is made up of both positive and negative thoughts.

There are many nights when my mind races. My thoughts tumble through the darkness as I anticipate all sorts of health catastrophes. At times my self-talk, the things I say to myself, can increase my anxiety, offer no solutions, and leave me exhausted physically and emotionally the next day. At other times, my self-talk helps calm me, alleviates my anxiety, and gives me a framework for solutions. Self-talk is a voice that turns on automatically in our heads. It happens to all of us and is completely normal.

We can interrupt the cycle of negative thoughts by practicing meditation and relaxation, using guided imagery, and making positive suggestions to ourselves. These techniques can be enlisted as powerful tools for gaining a sense of control over unpleasant situations and temporarily decreasing feelings of discomfort. They can assist a patient to believe in the effectiveness of treatments and the strength of one's immune system. The beliefs and hope we foster by giving personal meaning to difficult experiences give techniques such as positive self-statements life-changing power.

As Martin Seligman states in *The Optimistic Child*:

The basis of optimism does not lie in positive phrases or statements of victory, but in the way you think about causes. . . . Children who bounce back well from setbacks and resist depression believe that the causes of bad events are temporary.

Children can be encouraged to face the causes of stress in their illness and recognize that many of them are temporary. They can be taught to look at a specific situation, develop a way to approach the problem, and think of a solution.

The effectiveness of positive statements does not lie in simply reciting them. It lies in the beliefs one has regarding the message.

A positive self-statement is included with each of the active imagination stories in a context that the child can understand. The affirmation is embedded in the story several times to help the child learn it. When a child has mastery of a positive statement it can be applied throughout the day and in different situations. Think, for example, of how we teach our children to say "please" and "thank you" with the expectation that it will transfer to other situations. We can do the same with positive statements. The following statements accompany the children's active imagination stories. They are expressions of hope, strength, and optimism.

I am calm and relaxed.

My day is filled with interesting people.

Unhealthy cells are easy targets.

My stomach stays calm and steady.

I breathe in comfort and peace. I blow out difficulties and problems.

Each day of treatment helps me become healthy.

I can go to a calm, pain free place.

It feels good to express my feelings.

I dream happy dreams.

I am happy, healthy, and strong.

I am able to make myself feel comfortable.

My breathing settles my stomach.

My body feels comfortable and at peace.

I feel supported and filled with hope.

I can brush away pain.

I am comfortable as I lie quiet and still.

I go to sleep easily.

The medicine I take helps my body heal.

The medicine I take brightens my body with healing.

I can create peaceful, happy, and relaxed feelings.

I am filled with healthy cells.

As I relax, my stomach settles down.

I feel confident and calm in new experiences and new places.

I climb up to good feelings.

My whole body works to help me be strong and healthy.

Radiation helps my healthy cells take charge.

I am strong and I have energy to enjoy my day.

My body changes and I am still me.

Healing is happening inside my body.

As you evaluate your child's situation, you may identify events that are especially stressful. You can design stories and statements to meet the individual needs of your child. Chapter 8, *"Getting Started — Recommendations, Guidelines, and Specific Tips,"* offers helpful information on writing stories and positive statements to fit your special situations.

MUSIC

Do you have favorite songs or sounds that evoke peaceful feelings? For me, the sound of ocean waves draws me to a place in my mind where I can begin to relax. We respond to sounds in nature such as rainfall, a bubbling brook, or the songs of birds. Soothing sounds and music can help us enter into a relaxed state of mind.

Many studies have shown that we benefit from listening to the melodies and rhythms of instrumental music, such as from the Baroque or Classic periods (Bach, Mozart). Instrumental music has been found effective in stress reduction as measured by physiological changes. Some of the measures of music's effects on anxiety/stress reduction include changes in skin response, heart rate, respiration rate, pulse rate, and blood pressure (Achterberg 1985).

In other words, music alone can help counteract the effects of the "fight or flight" stress response. By pairing music with the active imagination stories in this book, your child develops a relaxation response that begins as the music is played.

Setting the Mood

Using the same musical selection each time you practice relaxation helps your child become familiar with the piece and associate the sounds with the relaxed feeling in his or her mind. When this happens, the sounds themselves will begin to evoke the mood and feeling of relaxation (Gorfinkle 1998). One way to pair the music with a relaxed feeling is to play the music each night as your child drifts off to sleep. We have only to remember the soothing sound of a familiar lullaby to understand this connection between mood and music.

Music can be used not only to soothe us, but also to stimulate us to action. Perhaps a rousing march or favorite energetic melody, such as *The 1812 Overture* by Tchaikovsky, can be paired with an aggressive visualization to attack disease cells and to cheer on the immune system. Different music can be used depending on the goal of the imagery you have created.

In the book *Remarkable Recovery*, authors Hirshberg and Barasch state:

> Many researchers believe that music and art provide a way to bypass the "static" of purely rational thought and access deeper parts of the brain — the limbic system, for example — that may be the key to the mind-body healing response.

The limbic system is the part of the brain that communicates through feelings. Numerous tapes are available commercially that can be used at home and in the hospital setting. The *"Guidelines to Using Music"* section lists several musical selections that promote relaxation and provide a calming effect. See the Appendix for information on ordering titles through Inner Coaching.

THE FAMILY CIRCUS.   By Bil Keane

10-12
© 1998 Bil Keane, Inc.
Dist. by King Features Synd.

"Ah! Rain on the roof. My favorite
night music!"

HUMOR

When my son was a toddler he invented his first joke. He would say the words "tickle-pickle" and then giggle as if it was the funniest joke in the world. We would laugh with him because his laughter was contagious. Not only is laughter contagious, it turns out that it is also good medicine.

Laughing stimulates our heart and respiratory rate, increases circulation, and exercises stomach and chest muscles. Cellular changes occur in our bodies when we laugh. Laughing can boost our immune system, and at the same time, decrease the levels of "stress hormones" in our body. The research on laughter is compelling.

It has been found that endorphins, endogenous morphine-like peptides, are produced and released into the body during laughter. Endorphins are a group of chemicals produced in the brain. When these substances are released into the blood, there is a pain-diminishing effect sometimes lasting two to three hours. The discovery of endorphins has produced a large number of new studies relating to pain control. Researchers are trying to identify additional circumstances, in addition to laughter, in which endorphins are most likely to be released.

The Power of Laughter

In his book, *Anatomy of an Illness*, Norman Cousins recounts his use of humor to induce pain-free periods of time up to approximately two hours after ten minutes of laughter. He found he could mobilize his healing energies through humor. But how can we possibly laugh when we face serious, sad circumstances? What a challenge to incorporate healing humor into our life at these times!

At first, after a cancer recurrence, I wondered if I would ever smile again. In fact, I was astounded that life went on routinely for other people. Didn't they know that disaster could strike their life at any moment the way I felt it had struck mine? Didn't they realize how frivolous their parties were while I faced a life threatening illness? It was as if there was a mismatch between my life and the world in which I lived.

With time I refocused my perspective. I learned to integrate the disease and its treatments into my life and not let cancer consume me. After my diagnosis, some people greeted me very somberly. Some were teary and sad. At the time, those reactions matched the way I was feeling and enabled me to share my own emotions with others. But I couldn't stay in that sad place.

I needed to develop optimism and have people greet me with a smile. With time, I was able to smile with them. I could laugh and enjoy myself, all the while knowing the benefits I was activating both emotionally and physically. As I shared my desire to use humor as a step toward healing, friends found ways to send a smile my way.

HOPE

The previously mentioned stepping stones all have research data to demonstrate their effectiveness in helping a person cope with crisis. Another essential element in coping with illness is *hope*. How does one measure hope? It is an intangible belief that we hold.

There is always reason to hope, and that does not mean we are in a state of denial about the seriousness of disease. No matter what the circumstances of our physical health, we have opportunities to look for special moments that enrich our lives. To have hope means we are open to healing and to a greater understanding of Spirit, our minds, and our bodies.

Elizabeth Clark states in *You Have the Right to be Hopeful:*

Hope is a way of thinking, feeling and acting. Hope is a prerequisite for action. Hope is flexible and remains open to various possibilities and the necessity to change the desired outcome as the reality changes. These aspects of hope emphasize how important hope is for living with a serious illness.

In the moments after my diagnosis, as I questioned my doctor about my prognosis, the most important answer he gave was his firm statement that he "always has hope." I didn't need statistics at that moment. I needed hope.

Choosing Hope During Difficult Times

When I was a little girl, I always wanted a rock tumbler. A friend of mine in grade school had one and I thought it was so cool to put regular looking little stones into the tumbler, plug it in and let the stones spin. After several days, when the tumbler was opened up, I saw the most surprising change. The pebbles that once had looked like plain, old regular pebbles now had a shiny, polished look. They were beautiful.

The first time I saw this happen I thought it was a trick and that the polished stones were not the same ones that had started out in the tumbler. I thought perhaps my friend had taken out the regular pebbles and replaced them with the shiny ones. But it was not a trick. The pebbles were the same ones. The magic was in the endless tumbling, tossing motion that buffed each stone as they spun around for days. Yet, there was one more detail to the magic. It was grit. A special powder was added to the stones in the tumbler.

When I am sick I sometimes feel like my life has been dropped into a rock tumbler. I feel as though I'm being jumbled and tumbled and bounced around. I feel off-balance, not sure which direction is up. I certainly experience the "grit" associated with disease in my life.

Often, there does not seem to be a good reason why we experience topsy-turvy times in our lives. If we think about the action of a rock tumbler and compare it to the unsettling times in our lives, we can understand how difficulties buff and polish us and bring out the true beauty within us.

I do not know how cancer will affect my future. I do not know if I will face it again, and if I do, whether my body will once again be able to put the disease into remission. I do not know if I will die from this disease. Perhaps you have the same concerns in your heart about your child.

We do not know what will occur in the future, but we can choose to be on a healing path. We can use the grit of difficult situations to polish life. We can embrace hope.

HOPE IS A CHOICE

By Mary Soergel

Hope is an attitude pregnant with healing, delivering peace to my inner being.

Hope is a surgeon for the damaged heart of my faith, bypassing the questions of my mind.

Hope pulls out the earplugs of my doubt with a gentle hand, opening my ears to healing voices.

Hope is like a mother hen who gathers her chicks together under her wings of love, teaching me what food is healthy and what food will choke me.

Hope sends me out to find other chicks who need a mother.

Hope's warm breath blows on the dark glasses of my fear, misting them, forcing me to choose.

Will I wipe them off, put them on again, continue to grope through the haze?

Will all of my days be clouded and dark?

Or will I drop fear's glasses on hard ground, crush them under my heel, and follow the bright light of hope's possibilities?

It's my choice.

Mary Soergel has survived cancer twice, her own and that of her son, Scott, who died in 1975. Her book, *Sing a Gentle Breeze*, the story of his struggle, was published in 1977.

PUTTING IT ALL TOGETHER

When one door of happiness closes, another opens, but often we look so long at the closed door that we do not see the one that has been opened for us.
—Helen Keller

There are many additional approaches to the ones addressed in this book that can elicit relaxation. You can find many resources available for learning about other methods. It is helpful to explore complementary methods and provide a variety of resources for yourself and your child. I do not think our plates can be too full when we sample the resources available for stress management.

If our path is going to lead us anywhere it must be built with more than one stone; otherwise, we will be standing still.

Chapter 4

BUILDING A TEAM

When your child is facing treatment, many new people enter your life. Your health care team will encompass specialists and support staff from different departments within the hospital and clinic. Coordinating the communication between your team members requires some attention. Taking good notes helps a lot!

Above all, your child needs the help of someone who can be objective and who understands the illness. A person is needed who has a vision for the long-term as well as a feel for the day-to-day concerns. Your child needs an advocate who is able to coordinate with, consult, and question the medical staff regarding plans for him or her. Your child needs the help of an adult, a coach, to learn to use a wide variety of coping strategies.

A coach's job can be thought of as analogous to that of the coach of an athletic team. When coaching a sport, the coach has a certain level of objectivity regarding the event and the competition. A good coach can see the "playing field" and has a broad perspective in regard to goals. The coach senses the rhythm of the game and knows when it is time to change game plans. When needed, the coach has the ear of the ref and can debate any of the calls that are made. It's part of the coach's job to motivate as well as to teach.

Using a sports analogy highlights the need for using a team approach for support and management during difficult times in our lives. The term "coach" is used because it is inclusive of anyone in your child's life who is able to support and teach. It may include any of the special people in your child's life. It may be a parent, a family member, a professional hospital worker, or anyone else who is able to focus on the intense experiences that accompany illness. As manager/coach of your child's support team, you can call in the people you need and enlist their help. You can be an advocate for your family's needs.

The concept of "coach" allows parents a needed flexibility in knowing others can help to support their child if necessary. Parents are coping with many responsibilities during times of illness and should realize that they can share the commitment of coaching with other caring adults.

Choosing the word "coach" is also significant because it allows your child to develop the ability to become his or her own coach. Your child can internalize what he or she has learned and build personal confidence in using relaxation and healing images for a lifetime.

Eventually, even when their coach is not with them, children who have practiced the relaxation methods are able to use internal coaching strategies to help diminish the sensations of pain and anxiety that they may feel about the experiences associated with their illness. It changes a child from a passive patient to an active participant in his or her treatment.

Perhaps most importantly, using these methods together opens up a way for family members to talk and share their feelings. It creates a special time for a child and coach to interact in positive ways around medical events. It offers the coach a powerful game plan. In this way, both child and coach gain confidence in their ability to cope.

The Role of the Coach

When discussing the role of the coach, a few basic assumptions are made. It is assumed the coach has these important values:

- An understanding of the child's illness and its treatments
- A way to talk to the child about the illness and build upon supportive communication styles that have already been established between family members
- Good communication with the medical team
- A spiritual/value system that adds meaning to these experiences
- A way to cope and care for himself or herself in difficult times

This last point is difficult to incorporate into the erratic, busy days and weeks of dealing with an illness, yet it is essential.

Support for the Caregiver

Each time I fly, I watch the safety demonstration that tells parents to put their own oxygen masks on first and then help their children put on theirs. This is another one of those times to take care of yourself so that you can take care of your child.

What if you are feeling overwhelmed and unsure of your ability to communicate with your child and/or members of your medical team? Perhaps you are unsure whether you have a support system that you can count on for help. The strategies, as described, sound good to you, but you're not certain that you can implement them. The onset of your child's illness has thrust you into a crisis and you feel pulled in too many directions and aren't sure where to turn. You feel that you are on a new playing field in a tough game. You may be wondering, "What about me? Who can coach me through all of this?"

You are seeking the best possible professional help for your child and you deserve the same. If you need help, take steps to get it. Don't go it alone. The hospital staff is equipped to offer help to family members. It can serve as a referral source to other agencies or organizations that may have just the kind of assistance you are looking for. No one expects a family to be able to step into the medical world and have all the answers.

A support group may be available where you can talk to others who have experienced similar stresses. It helps to talk about one's feelings and deal with them positively and openly. Support groups may be helpful for siblings as well.

Family members, friends, clergy, and health professionals can provide a safety net for families in medical crisis. Support often springs up, sometimes where least expected, when families express what is needed and what would be helpful.

REASSURANCES FOR CAREGIVERS

The profoundness of a child's serious illness may bring up thoughts and feelings you have never had before. The reassurances below can help you get through some difficult times. During periods of stress or self-doubt, it may help to reread this information.

- Nothing you did, or did not do, caused your child's illness.

- It is okay for you to express your feelings. Do not worry that you will make your family feel worse, or that you will make your child's illness worse, if you and your child express honest emotions such as anger, fear, sadness or anything else you are feeling. To express them and move through them to more positive feelings is better than stuffing such feelings inside. You do not need to adopt a Pollyanna attitude of always seeing things positively.

- Some parents feel that if they let their child see their sadness, their child will become scared or worried. You can show your feelings to your child and use words of reassurance so that your child understands what is behind the feelings. This will help to dispel your child's fears.

- Do not feel guilty if you take time for yourself to relax, to exercise, and to have fun. Eat well, maintain your support network, and take time to meditate or pray. Taking time for yourself will help you cope.

- A child's illness can place great strain on relationships in the family. Maintain perspective and work to keep relationships strong during these difficult times.

- Once a child is diagnosed with an illness, siblings can easily feel left out or deserted. Some parents have found it helpful to give siblings "special" alone time with either, or both, parents. Whenever possible, keep the siblings involved by giving them a role in caring for their brother or sister.

- Allow yourself to accept support from family and friends who offer to extend a helping hand. The help you receive can become the help you extend to others in the future.

- Do what you can to feel optimistic about your child's situation; your optimism will fuel optimism in your child.

- Your child's medical team is well equipped to help you. They have knowledge, experience, and compassion to know what your child needs. Your child will be well cared for.

- Don't panic if your child asserts that he or she is sick of everything and does not want to continue treatments. Listen and be supportive if your child expresses painful feelings. Be calm and tell your child that you will work together with the medical staff to get the best, most appropriate treatment.

- There will be times when relaxation strategies and active imagination stories won't be enough to calm and soothe difficulties. Everyone goes through such times. Hug each other, let the tears fall, and seek the help you need. Reassure yourself and your child that you will get through the difficulty together.

- In treating a serious disease many factors seem to change almost daily and many difficult decisions are required. Don't look back with remorse on difficult decisions you made in the past. You made the best decisions you could based on what you knew at the time. The same goes for decisions you will need to make today. You are making the best decisions, based on the information and intuition you have today.

- There is not one best or only path to healing. Do not feel pressured by well-intentioned people or articles that proclaim cures. Cures are physical. Healing involves the body, mind, and spirit and may or may not lead to a cure.

PARENTS SHARE INSIGHTS FROM THEIR JOURNEYS

The most valuable insights come from those who have "walked the walk." The following insights are from parents who found strength through strategies that they used to help cope with serious childhood illness. They offer their experiences and advice to families who are just beginning the journey.

When my son was first diagnosed, he was pretty sick and didn't want to eat, rest, or take all of that medicine. He always had a very active imagination, so we started playing a visualization game. We decided there was a war going on in his body, with evil monster cancer cells, and good guy soldier cells. Whenever he had to take pills, we thought up what they could be —- laser guns, tanks, bombs. He really felt that he had a role in getting well by supplying weapons and tools for his body's soldiers. By making up stories about some of these battles we reduced a lot of his anxiety about taking so much medicine.

— *From Dan, father of a seven-year-old son who was treated for leukemia*

Learn as much about the illness as possible. Our resources were the medical community and the Internet. Don't withhold information from the child. Explain the facts; admit when you don't know the answers. Treat your child as normal as possible.

— *From Todd and Marybeth, parents of a 5 1/2 year-old daughter who was treated for retinoblastoma-enucleation, a form of cancer of the eye*

My daughter was diagnosed with stage III Wilms tumor. I just feel, looking back, that there was absolutely nothing that could have prepared me for the news that my daughter had cancer and there's a possibility she could die.

— *From Tracy, mother of 4-year-old daughter who was treated for Wilms tumor, a form of kidney cancer*

The first morning in the hospital after our diagnosis I fell apart mentally. Our daughter was much too young to understand what was happening to her. A very wise medical student pulled me aside and calmly told me that the best medicine for my daughter was a positive attitude. From that point on, I made certain her day was filled with laughter and upbeat people. There were days that this was really hard, but to this day I believe it helped her fight the odds.

— *From Kris, mother of a 10-month-old daughter who was treated for acute monocytic leukemia*

Stay involved with the treatment and care of your child — help feed, change diapers, rub lotion, give meds. Keep your connection. It will help you deal with what is going on. Ask questions. Don't be afraid. This is your child and you have the right to understand what is going on. Don't worry about offending someone. Try to be positive — even if you are getting bad news. Be aware, but don't let the fear keep you from enjoying your child.

Appreciate your loved ones — serious illnesses help put things in perspective. It's okay to feel sad. Every time I felt down, someone would try to "help" and wouldn't let me feel how I needed to feel. I needed someone to validate my feeling and tell me it was okay to feel "gypped," to grieve for the healthy child we did not have, to be mad at God. I think this is okay as long as you don't dwell there too long.

My faith in God really helped me through this experience and it's far from over, but we'll cross those bridges when we have to. When we told our other daughter that her baby sister was born with only half a heart, she asked us if Jesus was still in Kaitlyn's heart. We said, "Yes, it's just a little crowded." We tell our girls that Jesus lives in our hearts and that he is always as close as our hearts.

— *From Jeanne, mother of a daughter who required open-heart surgery at birth and a heart transplant at nine weeks old*

The thing that helped our family was our faith in our Savior. If he loved us enough to die for us, he loved us enough to help us through anything. All along, he is preparing a place for our daughter in Heaven. He will know when that home is perfectly ready.

— *From Toni, mother of a twelve-year-old daughter who was treated for cancer*

My daughter was born with a kidney disease and we were told that she would need a transplant some day. When the day came it was really hard. It sure changed our lives. I look back to that day and thank the Lord that he got us through this ordeal.

— *From Tammy, mother of a ten-year-old daughter who received a kidney transplant*

There were two beliefs that helped our family. One was to have faith in something bigger — a positive force in the universe. Another help was taking control of what we could control and letting go of the rest.

— *From Cathy, mother of a daughter who was treated for rhabdomyosarcoma, a muscle tumor*

My son became ill on his second birthday. He spent two months in the hospital. During that time, a nurse told me that very young children begin to think of the hospital as their life. I knew I had to do something to help him remember home. So his brother and I went home and got every picture that was taken at home. We sat for hours looking and talking about the pictures. One of them was of the toy box opened with all of his toys showing. I believe this picture gave him the will to live again.

We knew that someday he might need a kidney transplant, so we began talking about it from the beginning. I told him that I was going to give him my kidney and pack it with all my love and he would be fine.

I told him that we would never lie to him and if he ever thought a doctor or nurse had lied to him, he should just come and ask us, and no matter what, we wouldn't lie. I also told him he would never have to go through anything alone.

The last few months before transplant were rough on everyone. We had long talks, yelled some, and cried. We always kept the communication open. My son received his dad's kidney and everything went wonderfully. He indeed is very lucky.

— *From Kris, mother of a son who was treated for kidney disease and received a transplant*

Take one day at a time. Remember how many people love you and are praying for you. I thought of other families who were going through worse than we were and that helped me. God gives you strength. Looking back, I don't know how we got through it. We had a new baby in May and my 2 1/2-year-old was diagnosed in August. We had to close on a new house the day we went to meet with the surgeons. Everything happened at once. We had no time to think. God helps you get through it.

— *From Valerie, mother of a daughter who was treated for Wilms tumor, a form of kidney cancer*

My daughter has needed a variety of therapies from the time she was a newborn. She doesn't complain about having to go to so much therapy because she has not known things to be any different. The hardest part of therapy is having to start over with new people, so if you find someone good, do all you can to stick with them.

When I look at my daughter I am amazed by all of her accomplishments and her positive outlook on things. She always brings me up when I feel sad about all of this.

— *From Joanne, mother of a daughter who has been treated since birth for congenital hypotonia.*

When my son needed scans he had to lie still for quite awhile. I thought if I kept him up later the night before he would be tired and might fall asleep during the scans. What happened was that he was cranky and grouchy and teary the next day and he had a harder time being still. I didn't tamper with his sleep schedule the next time.

One thing that was helpful for us was to always insist that any "pokes" be done in the lab. That way my son knew that there wouldn't be any surprises in any of the examining rooms and it was less stressful to move through the different diagnostic tests.

— *From Carol, mother of a son who was treated for cancer*

Treasure the people on your journey who intuitively understand your needs.

— *From Andy, father of a daughter who was treated for kidney disease*

Chapter 5

COMMUNICATING WITH YOUR CHILD ABOUT ILLNESS

Children often realize that something is seriously wrong with their health even before the official diagnosis is made. They have had symptoms that probably required more than one doctor's appointment and they have had a variety of procedures performed. Even if they have not asked any questions, they have picked up bits of information and, no doubt, are trying to understand what it all means. Parents need to understand their child's illness and decide how and what to communicate to their child.

Sometimes parents wonder what to tell their child. Most children respond to the manner in which the message is given to them even more than the actual words that are being said. Families who express hope, faith, and reassurance that their child will be lovingly cared for create a foundation for what is to come that allows their child to begin the physical as well as emotional healing process.

It is often surprising to adults that many children manage to brave the illness and treatments with determination and strength. Children who possess a sense of hope about their situation continue with medicines and treatments that may seem daunting. These children are able to tap into inner strengths. The family's challenge is to give meaning to the experiences associated with the illness and then develop their own way of thinking about the experiences and coping together in positive ways. Parents offer support, as well as coping skills, to deal with the challenging aspects of illness.

Facing the Unknown Together

In many situations, parents prepare children and ease their anxiety by talking about what to expect before an event occurs. The difficult thing about serious childhood illness is that most likely, the experiences are new to the parents as well as to the child.

The whole family is facing the unknown and needs to quickly grasp new information in order to make wise choices. Using the resources in this book, you can provide your child with language and information that offers ways to gain a sense of calmness and a measure of control over stressful situations. Many times we worry about things before they happen and then, when we actually experience them, we find out our worries were worse than the reality.

Depending on the age of your child, details about the illness should be provided that help your child understand what is happening within his or her body and the reasons why tests and treatments are necessary. If children are not told about their illness they may develop unrealistic fears that will be difficult to overcome. It is not helpful to simply tell a child to be brave without offering language to help him or her understand how it can be done. It is not helpful to tell a child an injection or test will not hurt when in reality it may.

Each of the sections in the children's book begins with informational text about some aspect of serious illness. The text introduces medical words so you can talk about what they mean in the correct context. For example, I was with a four-year-old who overheard the nurse tell his mother that she would be injecting a dye before the bone scan. The little boy looked around in fright as he interpreted the word to be "die." His mom had to do some quick explaining with many reassurances before her son was ready to let down his guard and have the injection.

Another child listened as her mother was told "We're almost coming to the end." The nurse was referring to the end of treatments, but the child worried that it meant the "end" of her and she cried that she didn't want to come to an end. Sometimes you will not be able to anticipate confusions that your child may have about vocabulary used in the medical setting. Encourage your child to always ask about things he or she does not understand, and assure him or her that it is always okay to tell you about worries and fears.

Learn what informational resources are available to you through the hospital or medical office. See the Appendix for a listing of many national organizations that offer resources for a variety of childhood illnesses. An annotated list of read-aloud books covering many serious childhood illnesses is also provided in the Appendix.

Honest Responses to Feelings

When a serious illness is diagnosed, children are aware of the reactions and emotions of family members and friends and they take their cues from them. It is understandably a time of sadness and fear. Honest feelings can and should be expressed, as doing so provides a framework for the child to begin to understand his or her situation.

It is helpful to reassure your child that adult sadness and other strong feelings are not because of anger toward your child or because of your child's actions or behaviors. Some children feel responsible for the difficulties caused by their illness.

Siblings, extended family members, as well as your support community are all looking for cues about how to react. As you talk about the healing imagery and positive statements your child is using it will open up ways for others to reinforce your efforts to cope. This is helpful to you and to your child.

Additionally, it is helpful to verbalize and demonstrate physical signs of affection. Holding a hand speaks volumes to a frightened child. To adapt a commonly used metaphor a bit, "A touch is worth a thousand words." Most children readily accept a backrub, a hug, and a kiss as gestures that increase feelings of calmness and comfort.

Discover the things that express tenderness, love, and care to
your child and use them lavishly.

A Little TLC

We can all use a little Tender Loving Care (TLC) during difficult times. The following ideas may bring some comfort to your child during hospital stays or times of recuperation at home. They are things your child can respond to by touching, feeling, tasting, smelling, or seeing during days requiring quiet activities. They will bring your child a sense of security, of courage, and the comfort of knowing he or she is loved.

I like the idea of reinforcing the positive messages being used in the active imagination stories by incorporating an item for children to look at or hold. When I started radiation treatments, I received two bracelets as gifts. I wore one or the other each day. When I put them on it helped me get myself ready to relax and use my visualizations about healing. The technicians commented on them, giving me a chance to explain how special they were to me.

Another helpful strategy for me was putting pictures of my healing images around the house. Have you noticed that when you are aware of something in your life you tend to see it all around you? When I was pregnant, it seemed that all of a sudden many women I saw were also pregnant. I never really noticed them before. The same thing happened when I was using active imagination stories to help me symbolize my healing. Lighthouses were everywhere, as were stars and starfish. If I told friends about my healing images, they found ways to send along a little something to remind me that they were supporting me, too. It helped me and I know it helps children.

For each of the active imagination stories you can look for an object or picture to remind your child of the healing images from the stories. Take the item along to appointments to hold onto or to tuck into a pocket.

Additional resources are available through Inner Coaching to support the messages in this book. An activity/coloring book called *Healing Images For Children Activity Book: For Times When Quiet Activities Are Best*, includes open-ended coloring pages that reinforce the positive statements and themes of the active imagination stories. Games and activity pages are included.

Another resource is the *Healing Images for Children Relaxation Kit: Activities to Bring Comfort — Toys to Bring Joy*. The *Relaxation Kit* is a collection of toys and activities that help a child anchor the positive messages from the stories through journaling, drawing, and playing. See the Appendix for information on ordering these resources.

What Can I Do to Help?

Many times, friends ask if there is something they can to do help. The following ideas may be suggestions to pass along to someone who wishes to do something to help you and your child. In most cases, each suggestion uses things you have at home. You may not have the time or energy to think about pulling extra things together, while a friend or relative would be delighted to do it for you.

"Prepare on a Bear": Use a stuffed animal to talk about what will happen during some of the new diagnostic procedures and demonstrate what part of the body will be involved. Demonstrate the approximate length of time a procedure will take. For example, for short procedures such as injections or blood draws, count down the amount of time it is likely to take. Tell the "bear" and your child what the behavior expectations will be. For example, will your child need to undress, lie still, or open his or her mouth? Discuss expectations ahead of time and possibly role-play the actions. Let your child know that in some instances he or she may be able to make a choice but at other times it will not be possible to make choices and he or she will need to follow the directions given by you or the health care provider. Give the "bear" positive feedback such as: *You made a good effort. Good for you, you used your breathing to help you relax. You made a picture in your mind and told a story to help you think about comfortable things.* Praise the effort. If your child has a hard time with a procedure and fusses or cries, comfort and reassure your child that you know he or she is doing as well as possible in a difficult situation.

"Pillow Pals": A hospital stay will most likely be the first time your child is away from home without being at a friend's or relative's home or a happy place such as camp. Use a permanent fabric marker and write the names of loved ones on a pillowcase for your child to use while away from home. Visitors may wish to autograph the pillowcase. Your child will be reminded of the people who are thinking of him or her. You may wish to use a blanket or T-shirt instead of a pillowcase.

"Star Light, Star Bright": Put a piece of poster board or large sheet of paper on your child's wall. Use a crayon to draw stars or buy a packet of star stickers. Each time your child receives a card, phone call, or visitor, put a star on the poster. Let your child know that each star represents a prayer or someone's wishes for their good health. Your child will have a visual reminder of the support system surrounding him or her.

"Comfort Bag": Assemble some items that you can carry to waiting rooms to distract and entertain your child. Depending on your child's age you may include pop-up books, hand-held computer games, tapes/CD's with a headset, a comfortable toy to hold onto. Other items may include a fragrance to put under the nose if a procedure has a smell that may be upsetting, a mint, gum, or sucker to change the taste after medicine, a ball or toy to squeeze during a diagnostic test. Your child may be interested in bubbles, stickers, or finger puppets.

"Good Things Happen": Take an envelope and draw a symbol of thankfulness on it. When good things happen, jot them down on a piece of paper and tuck them into the envelope. Talk about them with your child. Encourage your child to be on the lookout for things to be thankful for. Help your child see that where there are clouds there are rainbows. There are treasures even if they are hidden. Where there are tears there is also laughter. These things run through our adult minds but perhaps your child needs your help to put into words the positive, hopeful things that occur that strengthen you and give you encouragement.

"School Friends": School-age children may have extended absences and wonder about their friends while they are gone. At the same time, school friends may be confused and worried about your child's absences. Contact a school representative to coordinate communication between the children. Technology such as computers may allow your child to have contact with classmates and even "sit in" on a special lesson or activity. Contact the school nurse or school psychologist prior to your child's return to school so the issues of possible treatment side effects may be discussed with classmates. Your child may experience changes in appearance, behavior, and energy level and it will be helpful to have these addressed so friends can understand the changes.

"Mr. Sandman": (The sandman is the character who "helps children fall asleep." Children know the sandman has paid a visit during the night when they wake up and find a grain of "sand" in the corner of their eyes.) Sometimes it may be difficult to fall asleep. Consider using your child's sense of taste, smell, sight, or touch to ease into sleep. A warm cup of milk with a sprinkle of nutmeg on top, a fragrant sachet tucked into the pillow, a night-light directed on a comforting picture to look at, a special cuddly object to hold, or their own pillow from home can help in new places.

"Read Another Story": Listening to a story being read aloud soothes children of all ages. Friends, one of your child's teachers, or a brother or sister can read stories onto a cassette tape so your child will always have a story at their fingertips. Your child's friends, family, and classmates could bring a smile to your child's face by recording jokes and riddles.

"Strength to Stand On": Even if you must wear a hospital gown, in almost all cases you can still wear your own socks. Take advantage of the specialty socks found in nature stores that feature different animals. There may be a pair that matches the healing image your child is using, such as a turtle for relaxation, or a giraffe for a calm stomach. You can design your own socks using permanent fabric markers to reinforce a story theme.

Chapter 6
SOOTHING YOUR CHILD'S PAIN

Of all aspects of childhood illness, confronting a child's pain is one of the most difficult things for a parent to face. While dealing with your child's pain you are coping with your own fears and emotional pain as well. I have found that the expectation of pain, or the anxiety about possible discomfort, can really make things hard for our children and sometimes even more so for the parent.

My job as a mom is to protect my children. When I see my children face pain, my own sadness wells up in me because I want to stop it from happening. This is not always possible. Pain in children is difficult to think about. Yet, at times, there is no avoiding it and it is better to confront it and develop strategies to deal with it than to be unprepared when it occurs.

Navigating the Waters

When I was young I lived near a park with a river running through it. In some places the river was wide and deep but the section near my house was narrow and shallow, more like a brook. The river had a rocky bottom and in a few places the rocks stuck out of the water. I liked to make my way across the river by stepping on the stones. I would look across the flowing water and choose each step carefully, so I could try to make it across without getting my feet wet. Sometimes, when I thought I had sure footing, I'd discover the rock was covered with slippery moss and I'd wind up with a "soaker" when I didn't expect it. In other places I realized there were no rocks to step on and I'd decide to go ahead and wade in and get my shoes wet. The challenge was getting to the other side. Sometimes I just had to get in and get wet in order to cross.

I started to think about my experiences in crossing the river when I was being treated for cancer. Sometimes in the treatment of a disease, there is no way to avoid anxiety, uncertainty, or pain. You just have to understand that you will need to step into the water and get wet. At other times, with planning and careful footwork, it is possible to stay above the pain and make your way across the river.

When parents see their child in pain, they can give the message that there are ways to be able to get through the difficulty. It is the family's job to give meaning to this difficult experience and then help their child sort through the reasons for the pain. Whenever possible, focusing on how a test or treatment will ultimately be helpful can help parent and child to not be overcome by the process. Your child can be reassured that there are many ways to approach pain control.

Working with Words

The interpretation of pain varies among people, so it is helpful for your child to develop a way to express what he or she is feeling. Since your child's illness affects your whole family you can develop a family way to talk about pain. You can become as comfortable and matter of fact talking about this topic as you are when talking about other family matters. You can develop a family language that describes what the pain feels like, how much it hurts, and most importantly, expresses a sense of hopefulness and confidence that there are a variety of ways to effectively deal with discomfort.

A child with a vocabulary to describe pain can communicate in an effective way so parents and medical staff can respond appropriately. Asking your child questions such as the following will help to organize your child's thoughts to be able to communicate effectively:

Where do you feel the pain? When did it begin? Is it constant or does it come and go? How long does it last? What does it feel like — dull? sharp? throbbing? Does it increase or decrease with activity? What have you tried for relief? What helped or did not help? How would you rate it?

Charting Pain

Rating scales are often used to help children describe painful sensations. For example, a scale from 0 to 5 provides a way to compare the intensities of different episodes of discomfort. To teach a child how to use a rating scale, talk about past experiences and assign them a spot on your scale. Choose events that have happened to your child and decide together where they would fall on a scale between 0 and 5. You might start by talking about events such as pinching a finger, falling and skinning a knee, or getting an injection and matching them to a face and number below. By doing this, your child will develop a way to compare the intensity of painful experiences. This will help others understand what he or she is feeling. A scale using starfish faces is printed in the children's section.

Pain Relief Methods

Quite a few of the active imagination stories in the children's section offer ways to deal with painful experiences. The *"Stories for Helping with Painful Sensations"* give parents and children possibilities for working through discomfort. In addition, the following techniques can be used alone or along with pain medicines prescribed by your physician. Parents will recognize that these approaches are not reserved for pain and serious illness. They are used very naturally in many parenting situations. These common parenting tools are enhanced and deepened through regular practice and use.

Distraction is a pain relief method that takes attention away from the pain. You use this method each time you rock your child, or read a pop-up book, or play a video game, for example.

Active Imagination is a method of pain relief that uses mental images produced by memory or imagination. Your child can be asked to recall a comfortable feeling, or being in a safe or favorite place, and then bring those feelings into the present. Certain images may reduce pain both during imagery and for hours afterwards. You use this method each time you ask your child to "remember when" and talk about the details of a special, pleasant experience.

Progressive Muscle Relaxation is a method used to diminish pain or keep it from getting worse by reducing tension in the muscles. Progressive muscle relaxation is achieved through attending to each muscle group with a suggestion to tense and then relax each muscle throughout the body. It can help a person fall asleep, reduce anxiety, give more energy, and make other pain relief methods work more effectively. For example, it is less painful to get an injection in a muscle that is relaxed than one that is tense. You encourage relaxation when your rub your child's back, massage muscles, and use calming music.

Skin Stimulation is the use of pressure, friction, temperature change, or chemical substances to excite the nerve endings in the skin. Skin stimulation alters the flow of blood to the affected area. This method is used when we put an ice pack on a bump, or a hot water bottle on a cramp, or rub a sore muscle.

Children take cues from the adults in their lives and will be aware of the reactions of their caregivers. Caregivers need to keep their pain separate from their child's. I am absolutely phobic about dentists, yet my children's appointments have all been painless. I make a conscious effort not to color their experiences with my anxiety. If you wince before your child gets a shot you can predict that your child will tense up and will expect to have pain. You can use relaxation and imagery right along with your child. You will both feel better.

Chapter 7

EXPERIENCING RELAXATION
TECHNIQUES FOR COACHES

We have focused on using relaxation techniques with children, but Progressive Muscle Relaxation (PMR) and active imagination are appropriate for all ages. This chapter teaches you how to use each technique in your own life and then gives you guidelines on how to teach the same procedures to your child.

The following two scripts are provided to help adults access the relaxation response. These scripts give the coach personal experiences with relaxation, breathing, active imagination, and positive statements. These are the same strategies that your child will be using.

The **PMR** script is a helpful method for reducing stress throughout the body. **The Lake** is an active imagination script with a positive self-statement.

To be most effective, the stories should be read enough times for you to "know" them and be able to retell them to yourself whenever you want to relax. This will enable you to use the technique in various settings. Adjust the scripts to make them more meaningful to you. Personalize them by adding or deleting details.

Another way to use them is to make your own recordings of the scripts to help you incorporate the stress reduction methods into your own day. You will find it will be more effective if you can listen and relax, rather than read from the book as you try to relax.

If you make your own recording, select peaceful background music to play softly as you read the words of the script onto a tape. Read the script at a slow, calm pace and include pauses that are long enough to give you time to relax and create pictures in your mind. Consider giving your child the opportunity to help and support you by asking him or her to read the scripts to you. Your child might feel grateful to have a way to feel helpful.

The **PMR** script, accompanied by guitar music, is available on cassette tape for purchase from Inner Coaching. See the Appendix for information on ordering the **Relaxation and Success Imagery** tape.

PROGRESSIVE MUSCLE RELAXATION SCRIPT

Coaching Notes: *In this exercise you will practice relaxing your body by tensing and then releasing tension in your muscles. Attention will be focused on your awareness of the contrasting feelings of tension and relaxation. Play soft, relaxing music in the background as you read the script.*

Positive Statement: "I am calm and relaxed."

Find a quiet, comfortable place for yourself. Begin by thinking about relaxing. Recall a time when you have been relaxed and remember how good it felt. Just thinking about relaxation sets the mood for relaxation. Close your eyes gently, or focus on a picture or spot near you.

Listen to the music. Go with the rhythm of the music and relax. Music is healing and relaxing. Let the music take you wherever you would like to be.

As your breathing slows down, you begin to slow down. Take a deep, cleansing breath that expands your upper chest, your lungs, and your abdomen. Hold it for a moment. Feel the tension in your lungs and stomach. Then, release the breath and relax. With each breath, the feeling of relaxation deepens.

Let peace move through your body. Your heart rate is slowing down; your breathing is slowing down. All the systems in your body are relaxing. With each breath, feel more relaxation. Listen, and relax.

Begin to release muscle tension throughout your body by beginning with your head. Focus on your scalp and facial muscles. Tighten the muscles in your face. Hold for a moment. Now, release the tension in your forehead and eyebrows. Smooth out the muscles in your face.

As you are breathing in and breathing out, think of releasing all the tension in your head. Relax your jaw and let it drop slightly. Next, relax your tongue and lips. Your scalp, forehead, facial muscles, jaw and tongue relax even more.

Continue listening to the music as your body eases into relaxation. Allow the relaxation to proceed through your body. You may notice your eyelids feeling heavier and heavier as the relaxation progresses down your neck. Your neck muscles are relaxing and the feeling flows down into your shoulders and melts down into your arms.

Tighten the muscles in your hands and arms. Hold for a few moments then release. You may notice a feeling of heaviness in your arms that is spreading to your hands and fingers. Your hands are relaxed and warm. Your arms, hands, and fingers are getting heavier and heavier with the comfortable feeling that comes with relaxation. You may experience a tingling sensation in your fingers or a feeling of floating. If there are any spots of tension, warm those areas until they relax.

Pull your shoulders toward your ears and hold the tension for a moment. Release the tension and allow the relaxation to proceed from your shoulders downward to the muscles in your back. Let any tightness drain from your back and chest. Feel your lower back loosening.

Contract the muscles in your stomach. Hold the tightness for a moment. Relax the muscles in your stomach as you breathe in and out slowly. Let go and be calm. Feel free and relaxed. You may notice a heavy feeling of sinking down through the chair or bed.

Imagine sinking deeper and deeper as you gently breathe in and out. Imagine a pure white light coming into your body and scanning for any tension. The light surrounds any tension and takes it down through your feet and out of your body. With each breath, the white light helps you eliminate tension and helps you relax.

Curl your toes and tighten the muscles in your legs. Hold for a moment and then release the tension. The feeling of relaxation proceeds through your shins, ankles, and feet. Your legs feel heavy and relaxed.

Imagine now, a place free of tension, free of anxiety, and free of worry. Picture yourself in this place and think of it as a place of departure. Imagine a staircase or an escalator. As you step down, you become more deeply relaxed.

Go down the steps and count down from ten, then to nine. Your eyelids feel heavier and heavier, as if a weight were attached to them. Think of the effort that it would take to open your eyes. You choose to keep them closed. Go down to eight, then to seven. You are feeling more relaxed with each step. Your arms and legs are relaxed and heavy, as if weights were attached to them. You are now at step six, now five, and deeper to four.

With each step you are going deeper and deeper into relaxation. Gliding down to three, to two, and all the way down to one. Step off the stairs or escalator.

Now imagine being in a special place where you feel comfortable and safe. You feel loved and warm. You feel alive and in tune with your deepest self. Become aware of your senses as you look around your special place. Think about what you see, what you feel, what you hear, and the smells that come to you.

In this special place make a resolution to become more positive with yourself and with others around you. See yourself being positive and repeat to yourself with your inner voice, "I am positive minded. I give myself positive messages.

I rise above obstacles. Within me is a continual source of healing."

"Within me is peace and healing. I am calm. I learn from crisis. I set goals. I see myself becoming successful. I take care of my body. I eat nutritious food. I practice good health habits. I have energy for the tasks I need to do. I see my goal clearly and I bring together all of my potential to achieve my goal."

"In my mind's eye, I see myself as calm and relaxed. I say **'calm and relax'** when I need to focus on a task. **I am calm and relaxed**, become key words to say to myself."

"I take a minute to get in touch with this relaxed state. I give myself any other important messages or images. I take the time to drift with the winds of change."

"Now, I see myself coming back to the staircase or escalator. Before I step back on I know I can leave here whatever I choose and bring back whatever I choose. I bring back my key words, '**I am calm and relaxed.**' I step onto the staircase or escalator and go back up from one to ten.

I'm at one and then up to two, now coming back up to three and four. Feelings of relaxation surround me as I go up to five and six. I'm at seven and eight, now all the way to nine and ten. I step off in the middle of a place of total ease and comfort, free of tension and worry, free of anxiety."

Now take a few moments to appreciate the good feeling that comes with relaxation. In a moment you will find yourself back in your room feeling refreshed and ready to carry on with your activities. If you would like, you can choose to fall asleep, otherwise, open your eyes and stretch. Stretch your arms, your legs and your mind.

An Active Imagination Story

During the weeks that I received radiation treatments, I drove over 100 miles each day. Sometimes I stopped at a lake just off the highway to rest, or read, or think. One sunny day, as I looked at the water, I was filled with the image of stars sparkling on the surface of the waves. The stars on the water filled me with comfort as I imagined them to be each prayer and kind gesture that had been offered for my recovery.

Whether in oceans, rivers, lakes, or fountains, water evokes a range of sensations from calm and soothing to wild and raging. In this story the lake is calming but the energy of the undertow is strong. It seems an appropriate metaphor for troubling times when on the surface our lives may look fine but there are struggles going on inside.

You are free to bring your own interpretation to this story in a way that fits your needs. Encourage your child to do the same with the stories in the children's section. You will notice that the scripts include suggestions for using all of your senses. A **positive statement** is provided for you to use as an affirmation of your beliefs. **Coaching Notes** convey the goal of the script.

Precede each active imagination story with a few moments of relaxation and calm breathing. Be flexible in the amount of time you take as some days you may wish to spend more time becoming relaxed prior to beginning the story. Don't skip this part of the process. It is important to relax our bodies to elicit the greatest effect of the visualizations. Tape record the story or have someone read it to you so you can focus on creating the visual images in your imagination.

As I began using different healing images, I began finding pictures that symbolized the stories for me. My collection of pictures went on my mirrors, walls, refrigerator, and even the dashboard since I was spending so much time in my car. You may wish to incorporate a visual symbol to look at. Although the pictures we make in our minds may be similar to each other's, I believe, for each of us, they are unique.

THE LAKE

"I feel supported and filled with hope."

Coaching Notes: *You may be feeling like you are always rushing from one appointment to the next, to the hospital, to your home, to your work. In this story you steer your car off your regular route and take time to express some of the emotions you are feeling.*

Take time to relax your muscles and take calm, peaceful breaths.
Use the following paragraph or another of your choice.

Close your eyes gently, or focus on a picture or a spot near you.

Take a few moments to remember the last time you were relaxed and how good it felt.

When you are comfortable, take a nice, deep breath. Notice how the air fills your body.

As you breathe out, let peaceful feelings move throughout your body.

> Let the rhythm of music calm you.
> Feel your muscles relax and your heartbeat and breathing slow.
> Say to yourself: "I am calm and relaxed."
> Take three slow breaths and each time you breathe out, relax all your muscles.

You are driving to a familiar place, but this time you make a choice to change your destination and you turn your car onto a road that leads to a beautiful expansive lake. Make a picture in your mind of the quiet, tree-lined road. Look carefully at the scenery and see the green grass and leaves. As the scenery changes, you decrease your speed. You take time to look out the window. Your breathing slows as your car slows. Take even breaths in and out.

Now imagine opening the window. In the clean air, you can smell the trees and flowers along the road. Feel the breeze blow across your face. The sun warms your arm through the open window.

Park your car in a safe, shady spot and relax for a few minutes. Take a deep breath, filling your lungs completely. Now release the air, and as you do, release any tension in your muscles. Now breathe gently and easily. Listen to the lake sounds. Birds are singing in the trees. The leaves rustle as the breeze blows through the trees.

Now picture yourself opening the car door and heading for the water. As you walk, the smells of the lake greet you. You notice the fragrance of wildflowers and freshly cut grass. Breathe out the exhaust of the highway and fill your body with fresh air.

As you reach the beach, bend down and take off your shoes. Feel the warmth of the sand on the soles of your feet. Draw peacefulness up through your feet into your whole body. Feel your toes sink into the warm sand. This is a special time for you to reconnect with the beauty of nature.

Breathe gently as you walk along the beach. Let go of any stressful feelings that you are holding inside. You are alone on the beach and a feeling of solitude surrounds you.

Now, take another deep breath and fill your lungs and abdomen. Breathe in the peaceful solitude. Now, release your breath and breathe out the demands of meeting so many new people and making so many major decisions. Let the challenges facing you recede as you allow yourself these peaceful moments.

Gaze upon the shoreline. The gentle waves follow one after the other. They form a rhythm that you feel in your own heartbeat and breathing. Pace your heartbeat and your breathing to the slow, rhythmic pattern of wave upon wave.

Walk along the water's edge and be filled with peace and solitude. Let worries and fears wash away. If you have tears to shed, let them join the waves. Let them roll from you as the waves roll from the lake.

Imagine now, walking into the waves, and feeling the strength of the water against your legs. Say to yourself: **"I feel supported and filled with hope."**

The beauty of the lake fills you as you wade into the warm water up to your waist. Feel the tug of the current, the power of the waves. Notice that even in a setting that looks so tranquil there is an unseen current and you need strength to stay on track. Bring the energy of the current into your legs and feel it stream through your body. It is the energy that supports you, even as you push forward through it. The energy comes to you as each wave rolls in.

When you are ready, imagine leaving the water and walking to your spot on the beach. Rest for awhile as you gather in comfort and strength. Repeat to yourself: **"I feel supported and filled with hope."**

Look toward the water again. It is a sunny day and the sun is sparkling on the surface of the lake. The sparkles look like a multitude of shining stars. Each star represents a positive thought, prayer, or kind gesture that has been offered for you and your family.

You have felt the warm support of many people and now you can see it reflecting toward you on the water. The radiant stars are constant and unending. They flow toward you. Fill your heart with the beauty of the stars shining on the water. Repeat again: **"I feel supported and filled with hope."**

When you feel ready to end your time at the beach, take a deep breath and open your eyes. You feel light and peaceful. Whenever you need to feel calm and restored, remember your special place of peace and solitude.

Chapter 8
GETTING STARTED
RECOMMENDATIONS, GUIDELINES, AND SPECIFIC TIPS

This section offers an overview of helpful ways to use the stories and information with your child. It will give you a feel for details that you may wish to emphasize. It's the nuts and bolts of the program. Be sure to read this section before using the program with your child.

The **progressive muscle relaxation scripts** and stories cue your child to tighten and then relax different parts of the body. Preview the scripts in this section and **modify them if your child has physical limitations** that would prevent the use of any of the specific suggestions. Encourage your child to imagine tensing muscles and releasing tension even if not physically able to do so.

Inform your medical team that your child is using relaxation techniques. It may be a factor in his or her treatment. One study, using relaxation and imagery techniques with children with diabetes, found that the need for insulin decreased.

Check to see if your child will be having procedures other than those described in the section *"Thinking About Diagnostic Medical Tests."* Ask the medical staff to help you **explain the procedures** and define any words that might be confusing.

Many tests and treatments require a child to be still for several minutes. If that is difficult to do, the medical staff often recommends using a **sedation medication** to help the child stay still. Explain sedation to your child each time it is used. Many of the active imagination stories help with being able to stay still.

The stories about *"Helping with Painful Sensations"* offer a variety of approaches to deal with such a broad topic. All the stories **use breathing techniques.** When we have painful experiences, we tend to tense up the next time we're in a similar situation, so it is helpful to teach these skills to your child as soon as possible to avoid a generalized negative reaction to an experience. Use this section to help your child gain confidence in his or her coping skills.

To help you talk about **changes in your child's body** from the illness itself or as a side effect of treatment, read *"A Tree"* and add details to it that will specifically help your child.

The section on **taking medicine** contains general information about medicines as well as a section on chemotherapy. Ask for information from your medical staff, and then adapt the section to refer specifically to the medication your child requires.

The section *"Living with a Serious Illness"* suggests a way to **explain illness to your child**. Talk to your medical staff. Read other books. Even if your doctor has explained the illness to your child, like other hard things in life, you have to explain it more than once. Then ask your child to tell you their understanding of what his or her illness means. This will help you gauge his or her level of understanding.

Each active imagination story begins with Coaching Notes. The coaching notes preview the goal of the story and, in some cases, provide background information to help **establish the setting of the story**. They can be read to your child as printed or adapted.

GUIDELINES FOR USING HEALING IMAGES FOR CHILDREN

- *Revise or expand the information and vocabulary in the children's sections to include as much or as little detail as is needed for your child.*

    You want to be able to head off trouble rather than try to repair the damage from unnecessary fear. Ask a nurse if there are additional words that have been confusing to other children. Make a note to introduce them to your child.

- *You do not have to use the stories in any certain sequence.*

    In fact, you may choose to use only the ones that seem most appropriate for your child. It is recommended that the coach read through the whole children's section first and find where you want to focus your child's attention according to your child's needs and interests. You know your child best.

- *Coach your child through the stories.*

    Depending on the age of their child, parents can evaluate whether the descriptions and stories need to be read aloud each time, or whether their child will be able to remember them independently. The children's sections have been written to work both ways. However, no matter what the child's age, when a parent reads aloud, it is a special, comforting experience. Listening to the stories, rather than reading them alone, provides more opportunities for children to relax and to develop pictures in their minds as the story is shared.

- *Pace the stories appropriately.*

    When you read the stories aloud, read them slowly and allow pauses to give your child enough time to think of pictures in his or her mind. You may wish to make notations within the stories at the places where you need to provide additional time for your child to use his or her imagination and/or provide time for the relaxation response. The story can be extended or shortened to meet the child's needs. The setting and any details of the stories can be adapted to benefit the specific needs of your child. The goal is to develop your child's ability to use relaxation and imagery techniques to modify feelings and increase comfort.

• *Take time to practice.*

Spend enough time with a story so your child can remember the story line and make pictures in his or her mind of the images. Familiarity with the story allows the strategy to be used even when a coach is not available. Relaxation and rehearsal deepen the child's ability to effectively use the imagery. It is important for the child and coach to discuss and practice the relaxation methods and scripts before using them in the medical setting. Practice the feeling of a breath filling the lungs and stomach. It's different than taking a deep breath for a doctor.

• *Help your child relax in new environments.*

Realize that when you actually use the stories you may well be in a noisy, strange, new environment. The techniques will work in those settings too, but it helps to become very familiar with the stories and the steps to relaxation beforehand. The imagery is most effective when your child can become relaxed before beginning the stories. The amount of time this takes will vary from day to day and place to place. This step is important. Learn to recognize the signs of relaxation in your child. During each rehearsal, the cue words "calm and relax" are given prior to beginning the story. In settings with many distractions, using a picture as a focal point may be helpful.

• *Choose a "prop" to hold or wear that reminds your child of a key element of the story.*

A special toy or article of clothing can be paired with a story so, when needed, the object can accompany your child to a treatment to help your child use the healing images. The stories are written with imagery that children can relate to, such as themes with universal appeal, like nature and animals.

• *Change the stories to fit the age and interests of your child.*

The progressive muscle relaxation scripts are helpful for children and adolescents, as well as adults. The text and story topics appeal to children as young as four years of age through the teens. All of the techniques are appropriate to use with all ages. The images in the children's stories range from gentle and calming to aggressive and strong. They can be used as starting points for a child who may choose to develop a personal image to help achieve a goal.

Older children may be able to simply use a word, an image, or a physical movement (for example, touching the back of the hand), as a cue to relax or to help them remember the stories. The suggestions for TLC and loving touch can be adapted for all ages.

As you can see, the best way to use the stories is to make the stories your own. To help you get started, you can read the helpful and specific step-by-step guidelines that follow. Each of the guidelines refers to a child, however, all of the tips apply to adults as well.

TIPS FOR USING PROGRESSIVE MUSCLE RELAXATION

- Relaxation may be done sitting up or lying down. If lying down, put a small pillow under the neck and under the knees. It is a good idea to **practice in both positions** to prepare for different medical situations. The coach sits next to the child.

- Choose a time of the day that will **allow an uninterrupted time of ten to twenty minutes.** The more often a child practices progressive relaxation, the easier it becomes to achieve a relaxed state. With practice, the child will be able to achieve a relaxed state in settings that otherwise would elicit stress. It may take up to two weeks of practice to feel the first results of relaxation.

- Some children, after many repetitions, will achieve the ability to relax their bodies just by the association of thinking about relaxing.

- Find a quiet place for practicing. Dimming the lights may be helpful. Turn on music that is calming. Take a minute to listen to the music and **begin by taking several deep breaths.** The cue to "take a deep breath" does not mean to overfill the lungs, but rather to take a breath that feels like it stretches the upper chest, lungs, and stomach.

- It is best to suggest that the child's eyes be closed to **avoid distractions,** however, an alternative is to stare at the same spot or object throughout the exercises.

- As you continue the slow rhythmic breathing, encourage your child to **focus on a particular area of the body** and feel it relaxing. You can begin at the head and move progressively down the body, or start at the feet and work up to the head.

- To end the session, take a deep breath, **give a positive message** such as, "I feel calm and relaxed" and open your eyes. Take a few moments to appreciate the feeling of relaxation.

TIPS FOR BREATHING

- Take several breaths and **become aware of your breathing.** Follow the pattern of your breathing. Rest your hand on your abdomen and note if your stomach rises with your breath.

- Concentrate on a **slow, even breathing rhythm**. It may be helpful to slowly count, "In, one, two. Out, one, two" to prevent rapid breathing that could lead to hyperventilation.

- The coach can **breathe along with the child** to help pace the breathing.

- To begin a relaxation exercise, the cue is often given to "take a deep breath." Think of the breath as **filling your abdomen** as well as your lungs.

- The coach gives the child a cue to "Take a slow, deep breath, and **as you breathe in, tense a group of muscles.** For example, you can squeeze your eyes shut, or clench your fist, or stiffen your arms and legs as tightly as you can.

- **As you breathe out, relax your muscles** and feel the tension release. Use words such as warming, floating, and sinking to describe the feeling of tension draining from the muscles.

TIPS FOR USING ACTIVE IMAGINATION STORIES

- **Practice reading the stories** prior to using them so you feel comfortable as you read them aloud to your child.

- **Select calming music** to play in the background as you read the script.

- **Choose a comfortable time and place** as suggested above.

- A relaxation exercise should precede the active imagination story. **Concentrate on breathing slowly and relaxing muscles.**

- **Encourage vivid mental pictures**. Add or delete details to personalize and strengthen your child's imagination.

- If you notice your child's attention skipping around, say, "not now" gently and help him or her return the focus **to the in and out rhythm of the breathing.**

- Encourage your child to retell the story as a way to **anchor the positive message.**

TIPS FOR WRITING YOUR OWN STORIES

Parents and children can develop their own stories with scenes that hold great meaning for them. Think about the effect that you would like to create and then picture a scene that will bring about the desired outcome.

- The scenes should incorporate strong, clear cues for the child to use information gained through the senses of sight, smell, touch, taste, and hearing. The greater the imaginative use of the senses, the more effectively the story can be used to temporarily block out unpleasant thoughts or feelings. For example, **cues can be used that refer to imagining how something feels, or smells, or sounds.**

- Your **child should be the main character** in the story and the goal of the imagery should be established in a positive statement for the child to repeat.

- Comparisons can be suggested which **help your child see an experience from a different perspective.** Examples using nature and animals are generally effective.

- Children can **personalize** their visualization by using images that have meaning for them.

- **Select calming music** to play in the background as the story is being read.

- **Practice the story** for several days so your child is able to use the images on his or her own.

Commercial audio tapes are available that guide a person through progressive muscle relaxation and can be helpful for children as well as parents who may be experiencing additional stress in caring for a child with special needs. Parents and children may wish to make their own tapes with personalized guided imagery scripts to use independently.

TIPS FOR WRITING POSITIVE SELF-STATEMENTS

- State a solution rather than an avoidance. **State what you want your child to achieve** — not what you want to avoid. For example if you use the words, "I don't want to be nervous," you are setting down words that are connected with feeling insecure. Instead write: "I feel confident."

- **Always use the present tense.** Always state the desired goal as if it were an already accomplished fact. The subconscious mind responds best to the here and now of the present moment. Describe the specific result exactly as you want it to be for your child, not at some time in the future, but right now. Write "I am confident and assured," not "I will be confident and assured."

- **Give your child a key word or key phrase** that symbolizes the positive statement: Choose a word or phrase which calls to mind a strong feeling or vivid picture of what the content of the script represents to your child. If the script deals with belief in healing, you might use "strength." The idea is that the word or words you choose will create a strong surge of feeling and energy in relation to the goal you have described.

TIPS FOR USING MUSIC

- **First, try a variety of selections,** and when your child finds a favorite melody use it regularly. The music will signal a time to relax. Use it as background music in anticipation of medical procedures. Play the music as your child drifts off to sleep.

- **Select music that is long enough for your purposes.**

There are a wide variety of musical selections available to choose from to use as soft, background music when relaxing. Here are a few suggestions. The Appendix offers information on ordering music through Inner Coaching.

Pianoscapes (Michael Jones) — Soothing piano solos

Language of Love (Gary Lamb) — Relaxing music for classrooms, offices, or hospitals

Pachelbel with Ocean (Liv & Let Liv) — Canon in D soundscape with three variations

Bach Forever by the Sea (Solitudes) — Ten classics with full arrangements

The Fairy Ring (Mike Rowland) —Music for piano/synthesizer.

STORIES
AND OTHER
GOOD STUFF
FOR KIDS

This book is different from most other books because part of it is for adults and part of it is for children. This is where the part for children begins.

This Book Belongs To:

Tape your picture here:

_____

Add your name.

An easy way to find the kid's section is to look for the starfish at the bottom corner of each page. Put your thumb on the corner and flip through the pages. You will see the starfish in action.

PART 2
Information and Stories to Share with Children

An easy way to locate this section is to look for the stars on each page

60

MEET K.C. STAR

K.C. Star is a starfish. I met K.C. in a tidepool nestled among the rocks at the edge of the ocean. When the tide was out, K.C. looked relaxed lying in shallow water surrounded by snails, anemones, and other sea stars that were also residents of the tidepool. Gentle waves washed over the sea life and they looked peaceful as the sun shone down on them.

Then life in the tidepool changed. The tide came in. Time and again, waves crashed over the rocks and filled the tidepool with swirling water. K.C. didn't drown or get washed away. In the crashing waves K.C. was able to hang on tight to the rocks and stay safe.

K.C. is one of my healing images. A healing image is a picture I make in my imagination. I use my imagination to focus on a goal. I make a picture of K.C. in my mind when I want to feel relaxed and peaceful, the way the starfish look when the tide is out and the water is calm. K.C. helps me lie quietly and peacefully as I enjoy my day.

K.C. helps me in another way, too. When I want to feel strong during difficult, challenging times, I think of the way starfish are able to hold on to the rocks. I make a picture in my mind of K.C. hanging on tight when life in the tidepool gets challenging.

I use healing images to help me meet many different types of goals. The pictures I think about bring me comfort, strength, encouragement, and confidence. I think about lots of different images and you can too.

The stories in this book are filled with healing images and I know some of them will become your favorites. Maybe you'll think about starfish during times when difficulties seem to come at you like waves on the ocean and at other times when you are able to relax and enjoy times of calmness. You will find many more images that will help you.

K.C. guides you through this book. *Healing Images for Children* has sections that provide facts and information about illness. Those sections are followed by imaginative stories that encourage you to create pictures in your mind to help you reach your goals. The factual sections are illustrated with pictures of K.C. Star, while the active imagination stories have pictures representing the main ideas of the stories.

LIVING WITH A SERIOUS ILLNESS

63

Coaching Notes: *This section offers a way to explain cancer to a child. For children with an illness other than cancer, this section can be used as a model for conveying information as well as hope. The appendix provides a list of organizations that offer detailed information and resources about other childhood illnesses.*

Tips from Jacy, who was treated for a muscle tumor:

I was ten months old when I had cancer so I don't remember anything about it. I know mainly what has been told to me. I don't remember how I got through it other than I really wanted to live. I have never known the struggle with cancer, but I have known the struggle with the side effects. I believe that I, and anyone else who has lived through cancer, have survived for a reason. I can't say what that reason is, but I know that people who have survived through any catastrophe are the strongest people in the world. I want sufferers of any disease out there to realize that this is a lesson to be learned, not a punishment.

It has been hard for scientists to figure out exactly what causes cancer. They have discovered some things that cause some types of cancer. For example, researchers know that smoking cigarettes causes some people to get cancer that starts in the lungs. Yet, not all

people who smoke get lung cancer. Too much sun can cause damage to the skin that may lead to skin cancer. Yet, not all people who spend time in the sun get skin cancer. It is a combination of factors that seems to cause cells to change and become cancerous. To make the detective work even more challenging, cancer in one part of the body is different than cancer in another part of the body. For example, bone cancer is different from liver cancer.

Cancer Takes Many Forms

Cancer is the word we use to identify a group of over one hundred different kinds of specific cancers that affect different parts of the body. That is why there are so many different treatment plans, called treatment protocols, for different people. Doctors plan just the right combination of treatments for each person depending on the type of cancer that person has. This helps to explain why so many different tests are needed when a person first receives the news of cancer. Doctors need as much information as possible to put the right treatment plan into action.

All cancers involve cells that grow in ways that are different from

65

normal cells. Normal cells know when to make new cells, when to keep dividing, and when to stop growing. Cancer cells do not know when to stop. Once a cell becomes cancerous, it keeps making more cancer cells.

In some cases, these cells gather in one place in the body to form lumps called tumors. Tumors that start in the skin or in the lining of organs are called carcinomas. Tumors that start in connective tissue, such as bones, are called sarcomas.

Other types of cancer do not form tumors. Leukemia is a name for cancer cells that multiply in the bone marrow and then circulate in the blood stream and crowd out the normal blood cells.

It's easy to understand why it is important to get rid of cells that are growing out of control. If cancer cells aren't stopped they can damage healthy parts of our body.

Treatment is Carefully Planned

Once a person finds out he or she has cancer, a decision is made about how to stop the cancer cells from growing. Doctors are able to treat cancer in a variety of ways. Three of the common ways of treating cancer are surgery, chemotherapy, and radiation. Sometimes a doctor uses one of these methods and other times the doctor uses two or all three of these methods together. Your parents and your doctors decide what the best treatment plan is for you.

The thing that makes cancer such a serious disease and a challenge to treat is that when cancer cells leave the place where they first started growing, they can travel to other parts of the body. This is called metastasis.

Some types of cancer are very easy to cure, but even with careful planning and careful treatment, sometimes it is very difficult to stop cancer cells from growing. Cancer is a life threatening disease. This means that some people become very sick and die. Having cancer can be scary or worrisome, but it does not mean that everyone who has cancer is going to die from the disease. If you are worried or scared about your illness, it is very important to tell others about your feelings. Adults can help you understand things and that may help you to not feel so scared or worried.

When a person becomes healthier after being treated for cancer, he or she is sometimes called a survivor. A survivor is someone who has battled successfully against an illness or other difficulty in life.

Research Offers Hope

Doctors are studying new ways to fight cancer. Every day, in laboratories all around the world, thousands of scientists are looking for cures for cancer and new discoveries are being made. As scientists learn more about how cells work, they are finding more ways to treat the disease.

This gives us reasons to be very hopeful about the success of our treatments. I know I am. I am a cancer survivor and I have a heart full of hope for all of us with serious illnesses.

REASSURANCES FOR CHILDREN

- Nothing you did, or did not do, caused your illness.

- Your treatments are not a punishment and the disease is not a punishment.

- Your disease is not "catching." You did not catch it from anyone and no one will catch it from you; not your friends, your family, or your pets.

- At times, your family or friends may seem sad or angry. It is not because of anything you did or anything you said. They are expressing their feelings. You do not need to take away their sadness or protect them from feeling sad.

- It is okay for you to express your feelings, too. Do not worry that you will make your family feel worse if you cry or feel angry. It is reasonable to feel mad about the changes in your life. Do not worry that you will make your illness worse if you express your emotions.

- Talk to people you trust and ask the questions you are thinking about.

- The treatments may cause changes in your body and in the way you look, but you are still the same person that you always were.

- Even if you do not feel sick you may need to take medicine for awhile.

- There may be times when your family will need to wait in another room while you have a test or treatment. They will be okay and so will you. The hospital has many people who will take care of you and your family.

- Many people have hard things happen to them in their lives.

People get through tough times. There will be people in your life that will help you get through tough times, too.

- People care about each other. People are thinking about you and wishing you well. You are on people's minds and in their hearts.

- Even when things feel really hard, you will find other things that bring feelings of happiness and love. You will find things that you are thankful for. That is the way life is. There are storms and clouds and then there are rainbows. Keep your eyes and heart open for the rainbows.

THE REASON FOR THE STORIES

> **Tips from Maria, who was treated for cancer:**
>
> What is most helpful for my illness is the understanding and support from my family. I am lucky I have enough support.

In the next sections you will read about some of the things children experience when they are being treated for a serious illness. There are sections with information and there are sections with stories. Each of the information sections is introduced by a comment from a child who has lived with a serious illness and wants to share something with you that he or she has learned from the experience.

There is information about going to the hospital to have treatments and diagnostic tests, about taking medicine, and about the people on your medical team. There are stories about relaxing and feeling calm at times when you might otherwise feel scared or nervous. There are stories that will help you create healing pictures in your mind.

Scientists have discovered that our thoughts send messages to every part of our body. The things that we think about can affect the way our body feels. Learning to create healing thoughts can help you send helpful messages. The messages can help you cope with many of the things that are part of being treated for an illness. This is the reason for the stories in this book. When you take medicine or have a treatment, you will use your imagination to make a picture of it working in your body. You will learn to make pictures in your mind to help you concentrate on feeling comfortable during the many new experiences that will come your way.

Put Your Imagination Into Action

Many of the stories will take you on imaginary trips. The terrific thing about using your imagination is that it is always with you. No matter where you are, your imagination can work for you. You can be in your bed, your car, a waiting room, or just about anywhere, and you will notice that you are filled with good feelings and happy thoughts when you are thinking about things you enjoy.

When you listen to a story, you can put your imagination into action. You can add your own ideas to the ones that I have written in the stories. You can make up pictures in your imagination that will seem so real that you will able to see the colors, hear the sounds, and smell the fragrances. Thinking about the wonderful details of the story will keep your mind busy with good thoughts.

I have favorite stories, songs, and prayers that are in my memory from when I was a child. Just thinking about them makes me feel good. The stories in this book can do the same thing for you. But before these things can happen, you will need to learn how to do a couple of things. You will need to learn how to relax your muscles and how to breathe calmly and peacefully.

Relax Your Muscles

You may have heard people use the expression, "Let's sit down and relax." Maybe they actually are relaxing, but it could be that all they are doing is just sitting. There **is** a difference. In this book we will talk about *relaxation*.

It is very helpful to learn how to relax your muscles. For instance, we know we'll probably need a shot at one time or another. If you are tense, your muscle is hard. If you are relaxed, your muscle is soft. It's much easier to get a shot if you relax your muscle. That's just one of the ways relaxation will help you.

Breathe to Relax

Another thing we often hear people say is "Just calm down and take a breath!" What does that mean? Aren't we breathing all the time? It seems like people usually say it if they want someone to stop being "hyper" or to stop being angry or to stop crying.

You will learn a special way of breathing. There is a type of calmness that we will talk about in this book that comes from learning how to breathe deeply. You can learn what it feels like to have calm feelings. Being *calm and relaxed* is very helpful to us many times in our lives. One example is when we have to sit or lie quietly during an examination or during a treatment. It is much better to feel calm inside than it is to feel scared.

Find a Coach

To get started, you will need to work with a person who can help you learn how to relax your muscles, do calm breathing, and guide your feelings with your active imagination. We will call that person your "coach." Your coach might be a parent, grandparent, a nurse, a hospital staff member or any other special person in your life. You may even have more than one coach. Together, you will form a winning team!

Take Time to Practice

Each of the *active imagination stories* starts with a suggestion to take a few moments to relax your muscles and take calm, peaceful breaths. You will find a paragraph at the beginning of each story with suggestions for thinking about relaxation. Use the ideas in the paragraph along with other ideas that you have found to be helpful. Your

73

healing image will work best when you feel your muscles relax and your breathing slow down. When you feel ready, your coach will read the story aloud to you. As you hear the story, use your imagination to make pictures in your mind.

Pause long enough at each paragraph to give yourself enough time to use your imagination. Let your coach know how much time you need for creating pictures in your mind, relaxing your muscles, calming your breathing, and repeating the positive statements. Your coach may wish to put a star, (*) in your book at each of the places you want to pause.

Listen to the story enough times so you can keep it in your memory. The good thing about having the stories in your memory is that wherever you are, the stories will be with you. No matter where you are, you will be able to imagine a place of comfort.

Think Positive

Do you know the story of *The Little Engine That Could*? It is a story about a little train who had to chug up a long, steep hill. As the train moved along it said over and over again, " I think I can, I think I can, I think I can." And then, as the hill got steeper and harder to climb, the little train said with determination, **"I know I can, I know I can, I know I can"** and it was able to make it up the long, steep hill.

The train used a positive thought and said it over and over to help it reach a goal. This is called a *positive statement* and it works in all kinds of situations. Each of the stories in this book starts with a positive statement that you can say over and over to yourself either out loud or inside your head.

Don't be disappointed if it takes a few tries before it works. It will take some practice. Practice with your coach and then try it on your own. Soon you will know many ways to create just the right stories that will help you face many challenges. I know you can, I know you can, I know you can!

74

You Are in Charge

If you want to change any of the stories, go right ahead. You may have ideas that will work better for you. Use your imagination to think about things that help you feel calm, strong, and confident in your medical care. Share your ideas with others.

The more we put our feelings into writing, or music, or art, the better able we are to understand our experiences. A young man, who had cancer when he was 12 years old, drew the pictures in this book. Now he is 20 years old and he is in college. His pictures help me use my imagination as I listen to each story. You may wish to color the pictures in this book. Coloring and writing are ways to help us remember things that we hear.

You might like to make a book of your own. On each page you could write one of the positive statements, then draw an illustration and/or write your own story to go with each of the statements.

Some of my stories have animals as the main characters. It may make a difference in your mind if you picture the animal as "he" or "she." It is your choice to change the word to "he" or "she" to fit your selection.

PROGRESSIVE MUSCLE RELAXATION EXERCISES

> ## Tips from Emily, who needed to be in the hospital for many days:
>
> Each time my blood was tested, my dad sat next to me and told me to envision myself in a calm, happy setting. My father eased my anxiety with relaxation exercises.

You can learn how to relax your muscles using a method called **P**rogressive **M**uscle **R**elaxation or **PMR** for short. When you use PMR you will find it helps you in many different situations.

Some children like to listen to soft music and use PMR each night to fall asleep. Others use it during the day to rest their bodies and restore energy. This is important when you are healing from an illness. Children who need medical treatment use PMR to calm themselves before, during, and after procedures and treatments. Adults use PMR, too. You can use it for a lifetime.

RELAXING YOUR WHOLE BODY

Coaching Notes: *In this exercise, you will learn to relax by tensing and then releasing the tension in your muscles. You will focus on the contrasting feelings of tension and relaxation. If there are restrictions on your ability to tense your muscles, it is fine for you to tighten those muscles only in your imagination. You will still gain benefit from imagining muscle tension.*

Sit in a comfortable position with your eyes closed, or lie down in a comfortable position on your back. (If possible, play soft, relaxing music in the background as the script is read.)

Positive Statement: "I am calm and relaxed."

Take three slow, deep breaths and breathe out gently each time. Feel yourself relaxing more and more as your breathing begins to slow down. Let the rhythm of the music calm you. Feel your muscles relax and your heartbeat and breathing become slower. Say to yourself: **"I am calm and relaxed."** Listen to the music, breathe slowly, and begin feeling more and more relaxed.

(Relaxing Your Face)

Close your eyes as tight as you can. Squeeze them shut. Feel your face muscles tighten. Hold the tension in the muscles as you squeeze hard. Keep them closed and count to three: one — two — three. Good. Now let your eyes relax. Keep them gently closed as you breathe slowly.

Relax your face. Keep your eyes closed, but not squeezed shut. Feel the difference between tense muscles and relaxed muscles. Take a deep breath and now, as you exhale, relax your whole body.

Once again, squeeze your eyes closed and bite down as hard as you can, to increase the tension. Feel the tension in your face and jaw. Now relax your eyes, and jaw. Keep your face relaxed. Feel the tension fade away. Pretend that your eyelids are so heavy that it would be hard for you to open your eyes.

Now wrinkle your forehead muscles. Scrunch them up and hold the tension and count to three: one — two — three. Good. Now relax. Smooth out your forehead muscles. Let go of any tension in your face. As your face relaxes, feel the relaxation spread throughout your body. Take a deep breath and continue relaxing as you breathe out slowly. Be aware of this feeling of relaxation.

(Relaxing Your Shoulders and Neck)

Now, tense your shoulders and neck by pulling your shoulders up to your ears and tightening your muscles. Hold the tension in your shoulders. Feel the tension in your back, shoulders and neck. Hold that tension and count to three: one — two — three.

Now let your shoulders drop to a resting position. Relax your neck. Relax your shoulders. Relax your back. Now raise your shoulders up once more. Pull them up to your ears. Feel the tension in your neck, shoulders, and back. Hold it and count to three: one — two — three. Now drop your shoulders to a resting position. Relax your neck, your shoulders, and your back. Feel the relaxation as you rest your shoulders and neck muscles.

(Relaxing Your Arms and Hands)

Now, while you are relaxing, pretend you have a warm lump of clay in each of your hands. Squeeze the clay as hard as you can. Make your hands into tight fists. Now keep them closed and hold the tension as you count to three: one — two — three.

Now relax your hands and let them go limp. Feel the difference between tension and relaxation. Feel how good it is to have relaxed hands.

Now, while keeping your whole body still, squeeze your hands tightly closed once more. Feel the warm clay oozing through your fingers as you tighten your hands. Feel the tension and count to three: one — two — three. Good. Relax.

Smooth out the tension and feel the relaxation. You may feel your hands warming up as the blood flows into them. Your hands feel heavy, relaxed, and warm. You may even feel the air currents moving around your relaxed hands, and you may feel your fingers tingling as the blood flows through them.

Now, make your hands into fists, bend your arms at the elbows, and bring your fists to your shoulders. Make muscles in your arms. Hold the tension and count to three: one - two - three. Good. Now relax your arms and return them to their resting position. Let them go limp. They feel heavy, relaxed, and warm. Say the words, **"I am calm and relaxed."**

Continue relaxing while you let the air out slowly from your next breath. Relax your arms completely. You can relax even more by taking a deep breath and by letting go of all the tension in your muscles as you exhale. Enjoy the good feeling of relaxation. With each breath, you feel deeper and deeper relaxation. With each breath, your heart rate slows and the feeling of relaxation spreads.

(Relaxing Your Hips and Stomach)

While keeping the rest of your body relaxed, tense the muscles in your hips and stomach. Make your stomach and hip muscles hard. Hold the tension in your tummy while counting to three: one — two — three. Good. Now relax your stomach and hips. Release the tightness. Relax the muscles in your hips and stomach. Stomach relaxed, hips relaxed, legs and feet relaxed, breathing slow and relaxed.

Now tense your stomach once more. Make the muscles hard and tense. Hold the tension in your stomach. Now release the tension. Smooth your muscles. Relax your stomach and chest. Relax your hips. Eyes relaxed, face relaxed, neck and shoulders relaxed. Arms relaxed. Hands relaxed. Stomach and chest relaxed.

(Relaxing Your Legs and Feet)

Take a deep breath and then breathe out slowly. Pretend that there is a rope that runs from your toes to your knees. While keeping the rest of your body relaxed, pretend that you are pulling on the rope so your toes point toward your knees. Pull hard so you feel tension in your legs, ankles, and feet. Hold the tension and count to three: one — two — three. Good. Now release the tension in the rope and relax your legs, ankles, and toes.

Feel how good it is to relax your legs, your ankles, your feet and toes. Your legs, feet, and toes are relaxed and feel as if they are floating. Your breathing is relaxed. Let any tension float down through your body and out your toes. Let your muscles go limp. Let your body be still and say to yourself, **"I am calm and relaxed."** Drift on a gentle cloud. Totally relaxed. Breathing slowly.

Now push your feet down. Pretend you are stepping into sand and want to bury your feet. Push them down hard and feel the tension in your legs, ankles and feet. Hold the tension and count to three: one —

two — three. Good. Now relax your legs, relax your feet, and relax your toes. Feel all the tension drain from both feet, both legs. Let all your muscles go limp and soft. Think about the music as you drift on a cloud.

Take a deep breath and breathe out slowly. While relaxing the rest of your body, think about your toes. Now scrunch them up as tight as you can and keep them tight.

Good. Now relax your toes and feet. Relax your ankles and legs and notice them feeling heavier and heavier. With each breath become more and more relaxed. Think of being so relaxed that you feel yourself floating down comfortably and slowly through your chair or mattress.

Relax your muscles, clear your mind, and slow your breathing. Warming your whole body, let go of any tension and let your whole body relax by saying the words "calm and relax." **"I am calm and relaxed."** You feel calm and relaxed. Take a few moments to appreciate the good feeling of relaxation.

Now you are floating on a cloud. Your cloud floats gently to your favorite place. This is a place where you feel safe and loved. In this place you discover that you are at the top of a staircase. At the bottom of the staircase there is a beach. There are ten steps leading to the bottom of the staircase. Stand on step ten, then step down to nine. Enjoy the feeling of relaxation as you step down to eight, then down to seven. Feel yourself becoming even more relaxed as you step down to six; now five. Continue to slowly step down to four, three, two, and step off at one.

You see yourself sitting on the beach on a warm day. The sand is warm beneath you. The sun warms you from your toes to your head. Hear the birds singing above you. The warm gentle breeze feels refreshing against your face. You walk into the water and the sounds of the waves roll toward you.

A gentle wave washes over your toes and releases all the tension in your body. Breathe in, and feel the next wave smooth and relax your

81

stomach. Breathe in, catch a wave and rub the water on your chest, shoulders, and arms. Feel them relax. Bend down and rub warm water on your neck and face. Feel all the tension draining from your body from your head to your toes.

Turn from the waves and walk back to the sandy beach. Find a comfortable place to sit. While enjoying the warmth of the sun on your body, imagine being with someone who cares about you and who will always be there for you. Imagine the person telling you that you are nice to be around. Now, with your inner voice, take time to say positive things to yourself, about yourself, as you drift with the sounds of the waves at your beach.

In just a little while you will be coming back to your room.

Imagine stepping back onto the staircase, that leads up to your special place. Step up to one. Leaving at the beach feelings you would like to leave behind. Bringing back the memory of relaxation and your special words, "calm and relax." Step up to two, then three. Feeling relaxed and calm as you step up to four —five — six.

Feeling positive feelings about the people who care about you as you step up to seven, then eight. Smiling inside to yourself, step up to nine, and then step up to ten. Step off the staircase, back to your special place.

When you are ready to come back to your room, take a deep breath, and as you breathe out, allow yourself to slowly open your eyes. Stretch your arms. Now stretch your legs. Remember the feelings of tightening the muscles in your body and then relaxing those muscles. You are calm and relaxed.

QUICK RELAXATION EXERCISE

82

Coaching Notes: *This is a brief, or short way, to achieve relaxation. This exercise can be used in a variety of settings whenever you feel tense or anxious. You will learn to relax your whole body by using deep breathing, muscle relaxation, and the phrase,* **"calm and relax."** *You can use these words anytime you feel nervous or tense. Your body will respond by becoming relaxed.*

(If possible, play soft, relaxing music in the background as the script is read.) Sit or lie down in a comfortable position.

Positive Statement: "I am calm and relaxed."

Take three long, deep breaths. Feel yourself relaxing more and more with each breath. Feel your muscles relax and your heartbeat and breathing become slower. Say to yourself, **"I am calm and relaxed."**

Take another deep breath and hold it. As you are holding your breath, try to look up to your eyebrows without tilting your head upward. Keep your head still.

Now close your eyes and let your eyes relax. Slowly breathe out and say to yourself, **"I am calm and relaxed."** Let go of any tension in your body and allow your whole body to become fully relaxed.

Be aware of any tense spots in your body and tell any parts of your body that are not relaxed, to relax completely.

Now take another deep breath and as you slowly breathe out, tell your body to relax even more.

Once more, breathe deeply and as you breathe out, release all the tension from your forehead and the muscles in your face. Feel the muscles in your neck and shoulders and tell them to relax.

Notice your breathing slowing down. Feel the muscles in your hands and arms and tell them to relax. Let go of all the tension in your face, neck, shoulders, arms, and hands. Say to yourself, **"I am calm and relaxed,"** and feel your whole body become even more relaxed.

Relax your chest and stomach muscles. Tell your legs and feet to relax. As you continue to relax, say to yourself over and over, **"I am calm and relaxed."**

Now feel yourself drifting further and further into deep relaxation. You may notice a heavy feeling in your arms and legs. Each breath helps you relax even more.

Enjoy the feeling of being relaxed.

Take another deep breath and as you let it out, allow yourself to come back to the room. Open your eyes and stretch.

Remember that you can use this exercise any time you feel nervous or tense. Just take a deep breath and hold it. Close your eyes and slowly look up at your eyebrows without moving your head. Breathe out while relaxing your whole body and your eyes.

STORIES ABOUT RELAXATION

Now you have learned how to relax your muscles and how to breathe gently in and out to help yourself feel calm. Good for you! Those are very important lessons. Sometimes, all I need to do to be able to get through tough times is to relax my body and concentrate on my breathing.

At other times, I've discovered that I need to add a little bit more to my relaxation routine. At those times I tell myself a story and I make pictures in my mind. I let my imagination fill in all the details, colors, and sounds. I let the good feelings from the story fill my whole body. When I use all of my imagination, it is almost as if I can step inside the picture in my mind.

Doing this helps me ignore thoughts that worry me and feelings that are uncomfortable. I know they might still be there, but for awhile I put the problems in the background and I put the story up front in my mind. There are many stories in this book that you can use for times when you want to help yourself put worries or discomfort in the background.

Picture This

Here's another idea to try. Sometimes, in a noisy, busy place, it's a little bit hard for me to stay in my imagination. There are too many people and sounds that distract me. At those times, I look at a picture and I make up a story about it. Looking at the picture helps me keep my thoughts focused on the story. That way, if I am interrupted, I can easily look back at the picture and focus once again on my story. All of the stories in this book have a picture with them. Let your imagination add colors and more details to the pictures to help you concentrate on the stories.

Helpful Stories

The next stories, **"A Turtle," "Remote Control,"** and **"A Dragon"** will help you relax your muscles and use your breathing as ways to concentrate on good feelings.

A Turtle

"I am strong and I have energy for my day."

Coaching Notes: *In this story, a turtle leads you through progressive muscle relaxation, then suggests that your energy levels may be different at different times: times when you have little energy or times when you feel fully rested and energetic. There will be suggestions to tighten your muscles. It is fine to only imagine tightening any muscles that are difficult or painful to actually tighten rather than actually tightening them.*

The images in this story may be especially helpful before bedtime or naps, before anesthesia or sedation medication, or any time that you would like to feel relaxed.

There are many types of turtles. Some are so small that they fit in your hand and can live in a bowl. Others are so large that you can sit on their backs and take a ride. When a turtle walks on land it slowly lumbers along with its shell on its back. When a turtle wants to feel safe, it pulls its head and legs inside its shell and rests until danger is past. When a turtle enters the water it becomes sleek and graceful and can escape danger swiftly because it is able to swim and float with ease. When danger is past, it can poke its nose out of the water to breathe.

> **Take time to relax your muscles and take calm, peaceful breaths.** Use the following paragraph or another of your choice.
>
> Close your eyes gently, or focus on a picture or a spot near you.
>
> Take a few moments to remember the last time you were relaxed and how good it felt.
>
> When you are comfortable, take a nice, deep breath. Notice how the air fills your body.
>
> As you breathe out, let peaceful feelings move throughout your body.
>
> Let the rhythm of music calm you.
>
> Feel your muscles relax and your heartbeat and breathing slow.
>
> Say to yourself: "I am calm and relaxed."
>
> Take three slow breaths and each time you breathe out, relax all your muscles.

With your eyes closed, create a turtle in your imagination. Think about the size that you want your turtle to be, and then choose the colors and pattern of your turtle's shell. Take some time now, to make a picture in your mind of your turtle.

Pretend you are sitting by a pond with your turtle friend next to you. It is a sunny day and you and your turtle are resting on a rock warmed by the sun. The rock is on the edge of the pond. Lean over, look into the water, and see your reflections. Your smiling faces are reflected back to you. You are happy to spend time with your friend. You breathe easily and fill your body with warm, sunny air.

You and your turtle are ready to rest, so think of going to a cozy place. When you are in your cozy place, pretend that your body is inside a shell. It is quiet and dimly lit inside your shell and you are able to rest. You are very comfortable. Relax and enjoy your rest knowing you are safe with your friend.

Take a breath and then breathe out fully. Breathe in peaceful, restful feelings. Breathe out any tiredness. Enjoy this feeling.

When it is time for you to wake up, you feel full of energy. You are ready to go on an adventure with your turtle. Poke your head out of your shell, and listen to the frogs croaking in the pond and the songs of the birds overhead. There is life all around you.

Take a deep breath. As you breathe in, stretch out your neck as far as you can and tighten all the muscles in your head, neck, and shoulders as if you were a turtle poking its head out of its shell. Hold the stretch as you count to three: 1 — 2 —3. Now let the tightness flow out of your muscles. Let the muscles melt. Your forehead, eyes, nose, ears, and mouth feel smooth and soft.

Next, tighten your arms by bending your elbows and bringing your fists to your shoulders. Feel the tension, hold it as you count to three: 1 — 2 — 3. Now release all the tightness from your hands, arms, and shoulders.

Next, tighten the muscles in your lower legs by keeping your legs straight and pulling your toes toward your chin. Hold the tightness as you count to three: 1 — 2 — 3. Now, relax the muscles in your arms and then your legs. You are now relaxed throughout your body.

You and your turtle are ready to have a restful day together. It is fine to move slowly today and to be at peace on the rock by the pond. Your turtle knows how much energy you have and it knows you are moving at just the right pace for the way you feel today. Say to yourself: **"I am strong and I have energy for my day."** You look forward to today's activities. You know you will enjoy your day.

Repeat to yourself: **"I am strong and I have energy for my day."**

The two of you slowly and patiently move to the edge of the pond. Follow your turtle and imagine gently easing off the rock and gliding into the water.

The water supports all the parts of your body. Even with a heavy shell, the water makes your arms and legs feel light. The water is warm and you are able to float effortlessly. You have all the strength and energy you need to swim or float in the pond. Say to yourself again: **"I am strong and I have energy for my day."** Breathe in energy and strength and peace. Breathe out tiredness, pain, or fear.

Take some time to travel around the pond together. Say hello to the birds you meet as they build their nests. Swim past frogs sitting on lily pads. Dive under the surface of the water and visit the beavers building their lodge. There is much to see and appreciate.

As you swim through the water, feel it glide over your body. Paddle gently through the water. When you feel ready, head back to your rock. Slip out of the water and climb onto your special place, a place where you can sit in the sun and spend the day just as you would like.

When you are ready to return to your room, take a deep breath. As you breathe out, open your eyes. Take some time to wake up your muscles by stretching your arms, legs, and neck. You are filled with good feelings. Whatever you choose to do, you feel good about yourself.

Remember, whenever you need to rest, bring your imagination back to your day at the pond and spend some time with your turtle. The two of you can enjoy restful, quiet naps or you can pretend to slip into the calm water of the pond and glide along the surface together. Some days you feel like you need a shell around you to feel quiet and safe. Other days you feel full of energy and ready to explore.

90

REMOTE CONTROL
"I can create peaceful, happy, relaxed feelings."

Coaching Notes: *Each of us has a wide range of emotions and throughout the day our moods change. There are times in our lives when we can help ourselves feel better by changing how we feel about something. In this story, you will pretend to use a remote control, not for your TV, but for your emotions.*

Take time to relax your muscles and take calm, peaceful breaths. Use the following paragraph or another of your choice.

Close your eyes gently, or focus on a picture or a spot near you.

Take a few moments to remember the last time you were relaxed and how good it felt.

When you are comfortable, take a nice, deep breath. Notice how the air fills your body.

As you breathe out, let peaceful feelings move throughout your body.

Let the rhythm of music calm you.

Feel your muscles relax and your heartbeat and breathing slow.

Say to yourself: "I am calm and relaxed."

Take three slow breaths and each time you breathe out, relax all your muscles.

I magine that you find a magical TV remote control on your doorstep and you bring it inside. You are surprised to discover colorful writing on the back of it. The writing says, *"There are times in our lives when we can help ourselves feel better by changing how we feel about something."*

You are curious. You want to discover what this magical remote does, so you find a comfortable place to watch TV and you give it a try.

Begin now by taking a deep breath and imagine snuggling into your chair to relax. As you breathe out, sigh with a satisfied feeling, and let your arms and legs get comfortable. You are ready to try out your magical remote.

Begin pushing the button and slowly scan through your channels. What a surprise! Instead of seeing TV programs, you see stories from your own life! You discover a different story on each channel for feelings like happiness, anger, fear, sadness, peacefulness, silliness, seriousness, and all the many other emotions you feel.

Flip through the channels and find one that matches the way you are feeling right now. What is making you feel the way you do? What is happening in your life right now? Think about how you are feeling. Imagine your TV screen showing that picture. Add details to the picture. Think about where you are. Name some of the things that you can see, touch, and smell in your very own story.

Here's another surprise. You can use the volume buttons on your remote control to make the feelings in your body stronger or softer. Using your imagination, turn down the volume on your feelings. Slowly, feel the emotion become softer. The emotion is still with you but you can change it. You can make it feel softer.

If you want to, you can change again, and this time you can make the feeling stronger. You can turn the feelings up and down. Take some time to see how it feels to make a feeling softer and then stronger. Enjoy your show.

When you are ready to go to a different channel, take a deep breath. Blow the air out softly and slowly through your lips, then change to Channel #1 on your personal TV. Channel #1 is your Peaceful Channel. Imagine seeing a picture of yourself at a time when you felt peaceful. Go to that place now and see what happens. Notice the peaceful feeling spread throughout your body. Peaceful feelings are often soft and warm.

Take some time now to enjoy watching your peaceful show. Think about what you see and what you hear. Think about what brings you happiness and relaxation in your life. Say to yourself: **"I can create peaceful, happy, relaxed feelings."** Whenever you choose, you can switch to Peaceful Channel #1 and enjoy your peaceful feelings.

With your inner voice, repeat three times: **"I can create peaceful, happy, relaxed feelings."** Your thoughts help you create spots you can go to whenever you wish. You can create more shows on more of your own channels. Imagine creating a show of your own on Channel #2 and Channel #3.

When you change channels, remember that all your other feelings are still with you. You may have painful, or sad, or mad feelings. They are important too. You can make them feel louder or softer. Whenever you want, you can choose one of your channels with comfortable, positive feelings. Thinking about using your very own remote control helps you experience all your feelings.

When you feel ready to return to the room, take a deep breath. As you breathe out, open your eyes, and bring your mind back to your room. Continue to enjoy the calm peaceful feelings of relaxation.

Think about the stories on all your channels. Can you think of other situations where your magical remote control would be helpful? For example, if you ever have an upset stomach, you can make up a show that helps you feel better.

You may wish to take some time to tell someone about your shows, to write about them, and to draw pictures about them. All of these things help us remember and understand our feelings.

A DRAGON

"It feels good to express my feelings."

Coaching Notes *In this story, a dragon helps you express any of your feelings from anger to happiness. You are encouraged to express feelings in ways that are safe and that help you feel better.*

Dragons are not real but they are favorite characters in many books and fairy tales. Make-believe dragons can devour things. They can blow out a fiery breath. Some books have dragons that are friendly and harmless. Perhaps you have seen the movie "Pete's Dragon," or sang the song "Puff the Magic Dragon," in which a dragon becomes a friend to a child. This is the kind of dragon to imagine. In this story you will make-believe you have your very own dragon that always knows how you feel and is there to help you when you need to let out your feelings

---

Take time to relax your muscles and take calm, peaceful breaths.
Use the following paragraph or another of your choice.
Close your eyes gently, or focus on a picture or a spot near you.
Take a few moments to remember the last time you were relaxed and how good it felt.

When you are comfortable, take a nice, deep breath. Notice how the air fills your body.

As you breathe out, let peaceful feelings move throughout your body.

Let the rhythm of music calm you.

Feel your muscles relax and your heartbeat and breathing slow.

Say to yourself: "I am calm and relaxed."

Take three slow breaths and each time you breathe out, relax all your muscles.

Begin by imagining you are taking a walk along a path in an enchanted forest. The branches of the trees form an arch over your head. The sun filters through the leaves and makes little shadows that move back and forth as the wind blows. The shadows look like little butterflies circling around you. As you walk along, you whistle a little tune. The wind whispering through the treetops seems to say to you, "Welcome. I am glad you are here."

The path you are on has many curves and hills. It is difficult to see what is ahead. Whenever you come to a hill, you walk very slowly to give yourself time to peek over the top to see what is on the other side. All of a sudden, the hill you are walking on begins to move! It is the back of a dragon and you are standing near its head!

Imagine how surprised everyone would be to know you are standing on a dragon. Your footsteps tickle the dragon's neck and as it is waking up it turns its long neck and faces you. Yikes! You take a deep breath and hold it as you wait for the dragon to make the first move. The dragon smiles! You are so relieved, you let out your breath with a big whooshing sound, and you relax.

The dragon winks its big brown eye at you, and you feel safe. The dragon lets you in on a secret. It is looking for a friend. The dragon's skin feels warm and cuddly so you crawl to a comfortable spot on his/her back and whisper that you will be a friend.

When you have a friend, you can talk together about your feelings. Your dragon is just that kind of friend. Your magical dragon lets you take all the time you need to talk about how you feel. Sometimes people have feelings of anger or fear or sadness and it is hard to find words to tell people about them. Your friend understands.

You can be as scary and mean and as fierce as you want to be with your dragon. Pretend you feel angry and you feel like roaring. Go ahead and roar really loud! Now, roar even louder! Listen to your dragon as it roars with you.

It is okay to feel angry and to roar. Together you make a huge sound and you release your feelings. Buildings shake and trees bend from your loud noise. After you breathe out the angry feelings your body feels lighter and you feel calm.

Now pretend you are full of hot feelings of fear and you want to breathe out fire. The dragon joins you in your hot feelings with sounds that sizzle and whistle around you. Your frightening sounds even scare the animals in the forest and they take cover in caves.

Together you and your dragon are fierce and brave as you express your feelings. The sky turns orange and red from your fiery breath. After you breathe out hot feelings, your body feels cool, and you feel calm.

Now pretend there is a song in your heart and it is full of loud drums, trumpets, and crashing cymbals. The dragon loves this wild song. Thundering sounds burst from the two of you. The sounds are so loud they make the wind blow around you like a storm. The two of you are lifted up by the stormy wind and soar high into the sky. You bounce across the sky on the sounds of the strong music.

After awhile, the final notes of music fade away. You return to the forest. You breathe in and out slowly. Your mood has changed. You emptied out the loud, angry, hot feelings that were inside of you. You breathed out the crashing sounds, and now your body feels loose and you feel calm.

As you and your dragon look at each other, smiles spread over your faces. You both begin to giggle as you think about how fierce you looked to everyone in the forest as you flew through the sky. Reach out your arms and hug your dragon. Notice that now you are filled with happy feelings. When you are filled with happy feelings you feel contented. Breathe slowly and repeat to yourself three times: **"It feels good to express my feelings."**

When your journey is finished and you are ready to return to your room, take a deep breath. As you breathe out, open your eyes and gently return to your room. You feel refreshed and peaceful.

Remember that a dragon is an imaginary creature. You can create your own dragon and go on many different adventures with your friend. Whenever you want to return to this happy place, climb on your dragon's back and take flight together. Leave everything behind you. Fly with your dragon on a journey filled with all your feelings.

You are learning that it is important to let out your feelings in ways that are safe and that help you feel better. You are also learning that you have many different kinds of feelings and it is good to express your emotions.

Write about your journey, draw pictures of your special place, sing a song or listen to music to match your feelings. When you need to help yourself feel comfortable, remember the good feelings you had on your trip with your dragon and remember the good feelings that come from expressing the many different ways you feel.

THINKING ABOUT YOUR HEALTH CARE TEAM

Tips from Dana, who was treated for cancer:

It's okay to let lots of doctors take care of you so they can learn. It's okay if kids ask lots of questions of the people who take care of them. Kids need to understand, too.

Sometimes children stay overnight at the hospital. There are many reasons why a doctor asks a person to sleep at the hospital. Sometimes people need extra help to get well. At other times, a child needs long medical tests, or needs to receive certain medicines or treatments that can only be given in a hospital. Sometimes children stay at the hospital because they are too sick to be at home and they need the attention of medical helpers during the daytime and during the nighttime. Sometimes, but not always, a person stays at the hospital after having surgery.

There are many differences between your home and a hospital. A hospital is a busy place. There are many different sounds and smells at the hospital. When you check-in, you are given a plastic bracelet to wear with your name and other important information on it. Hospital beds have railings on the sides. They also have buttons you press to make the bed move up and down. When you need help, you press a button and a nurse comes to check on you. Hospital food comes to you on a tray from the hospital kitchen.

Nice to Meet You

One of the biggest differences between your home and the hospital is the number of people who come in and out of your room throughout the day and night. Some of them will come and go quickly as they do their jobs. Others will stop in more often and will spend some time visiting with you. Still others will work at jobs in other places in the hospital, and you will leave your room and visit them at the lab, office, or treatment room. All the people you meet are on your team and everyone is working together to help you feel better.

A doctor will usually visit you every day to see how you are doing. Nurses will stop in throughout the day and night to give you your medications, check your temperature and blood pressure, and make you feel as comfortable as possible. Nurses give your parents information about your care.

It is nice to have an idea of which people you might expect to see each day and what tests or procedures may be planned for you. Your

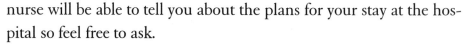

nurse will be able to tell you about the plans for your stay at the hospital so feel free to ask.

The next section in this book is called **"An ABC List of My Health Care Team."** It will help you understand how the people in the hospital will help you. When you have a visitor, or when you meet someone new in the hospital, you could ask him or her to sign your **"Autograph"** page. You will find it right after the **ABC List.**

Helpful Stories

The stories **"Aquarium"** and **"Ship Deck"** can help you think positively about the people you meet.

Another helpful section to read is the descriptions of tests in the section called **"Doctors Get Information in Many Ways — Diagnostic Tests."** It explains what you might expect if a test or procedure is planned for you.

An ABC List of My Health Care Team

101

Here are some of the people you may meet at the hospital. It is an alphabetical list of people on health care teams. If someone on your medical team is not included on the list, please feel free to add the person's name. Each person on your team is important.

This seems like a very long list of people, doesn't it? Your team will have some, not all, of these caregivers. Don't worry about meeting so many new people. You'll soon recognize familiar faces.

Write the names of the people who are on your health care team on the blank lines next to the titles.

Chaplain: _____
a member of the health team who helps children and families deal with the spiritual and emotional aspects of their lives.

Child Life Specialist: _____
a person who encourages children in learning, play, self-expression, and family involvement while in the hospital.

Environmental Service Worker: _____
a person who keeps the hospital very clean to help eliminate germs that can cause infection. Your hospital may call the person a custodian or housekeeper.

Medical Technologist: _____
a person who is trained to perform medical procedures such as blood tests. The lab tech looks at the blood cells under a microscope. Medical technologists are trained to run some of the complicated machinery and monitors in the hospital.

Nurse:
a person who provides day-to-day care. Nurses give medicine and watch the patient's condition. They have the most contact with patients and are available to answer questions or refer the patient to someone who can help.

Nurse Practitioner:
a nurse with specialized education who is able to assist the doctor in managing patient care.

Nursing Assistant:
a person who has studied to help the nurse give care to patients.

Nutritionist:
a person who helps patients get the best possible nutrition, in order to improve healing and maintain strength.

Occupational Therapist:
a person who specializes in maintaining a person's abilities in daily living, play, school and /or work.

Physicians: There are many different types of doctors. Here are some you might meet.

Anesthesiologist:
a physician who gives you medicine so that you will not feel pain during surgery and at other times.

Hematologist:
a physician who studies diseases of the blood.

Intern:
a physician who has finished medical school and is working in the hospital as part of his/her further training.

Oncologist:_____

a physician who specializes in identifying and treating cancer.

Pathologist:_____

a physician who interprets and diagnoses the changes caused by disease in body tissues.

Pediatrician:_____

a physician who specializes in the medical care of children.

Psychiatrist:_____

a physician who specializes in conditions affecting the mind and emotions.

Radiologist:_____

a physician with special training in reading diagnostic x-rays.

Resident:_____

a physician who has completed an internship and is continuing study to specialize in a specific area of medicine.

Surgeon:_____

a physician who performs operations.

Psychologist:_____

a person who is trained to help people during difficult times and frequently meets with families who have a child hospitalized with a serious illness. Through talk and play, they help people with their emotions and may teach patients about pain control methods.

Physical Therapist:_____

a person who specializes in exercises to keep muscles strong and flexible. The therapist uses methods to decrease pain in muscles, nerves, joints, and bones with exercise, electrical stimulation, hydrotherapy, and the use of massage, heat, cold, and electrical devices.

103

Radiation Therapy Technologist:_____

a person who is a specially trained technician who assists the radiation oncologist in giving external radiation treatments.

Social Worker:_____

a person who specializes in the emotional and social adjustment of children and families. Often, a social worker is assigned to each family to help them during their illness.

Teacher:_____

a person who coordinates schoolwork during hospital stays. Many hospitals have schoolrooms in the pediatric departments.

Volunteer:_____

a person who is not paid to work in the hospital. He or she works with patients in many ways simply because they want to help others.

Here is a place for you to add the names of other people on your team:

_____

_____

_____

_____

_____

_____

_____

_____

_____

_____

_____

106

AUTOGRAPHS

Ask visitors and your health care team members to
sign your Autographs page.

107

AUTOGRAPHS

Ask visitors and your health care team members to
sign your Autographs page.

STORIES ABOUT WAITING FOR APPOINTMENTS

Tips from Olivia, who has frequent medical appointments

It's hard when you have to wait for doctors. And if you need lots of doctor help, it's hard having to see them so many times. When you are waiting, get a book, because if you are sick you don't feel like walking around. A little snack helps. The doctor will come fast if you are really sick!

When you have a serious illness you find yourself spending time in waiting rooms. There are waiting rooms for doctor's appointments, waiting rooms for tests, and waiting rooms for treatments. Waiting can seem like a really long, slow time. Plan ahead so you can use the time in an interesting way. Bring activities with you that will help you stay calm and relaxed. You may want to carry drawing paper, books, crayons, small toys, a Walkman, or handheld games. When you are doing activities you enjoy, time always seems to pass more quickly. There will be times when you will be busy having a treatment or test and your coach will have to wait for you! Your coach can bring along interesting things to do, too.

A Time to Share Information

Sometimes if you do not feel well, your parents take you to the doctor to find out the reason why. But a visit to your doctor does not

109

necessarily mean you are sick. Sometimes you go to the doctor when you are well for a regular check-up.

Your doctor can learn many things from an examination. A doctor's appointment is the time for you and your doctor to ask each other questions and give each other information. It is a time to tell about any changes you have noticed. You may ask about any worries you have and you can share the good news about any improvements.

Helpful Stories

Read **"Aquarium"** and **"Blast-Off!"** to think about staying calm during the waiting time before a treatment, appointment, or diagnostic test.

Read **"Ship Deck"** for ideas about feeling relaxed in new places.

Read **"Peaceful Swamp"** for ideas for lying quiet and still during tests and treatments.

AQUARIUM

"My day is filled with interesting people."

Coaching Notes: *As you enter the hospital or your doctor's office, you often see people of all ages and sizes walking around or sitting in chairs waiting for their appointment. When you look around the waiting room, what do you notice? Do you see large glass windows? Do you see potted plants? Are there people moving about?*

Use your imagination to think about going to a medical appointment. Pretend the office is really a large aquarium and the people are brightly colored tropical fish. Using your imagination helps you have calm thoughts as you wait for a treatment or for an appointment.

Take time to relax your muscles and take calm, peaceful breaths.
Use the following paragraph or another of your choice.

Close your eyes gently, or focus on a picture or a spot near you.

Take a few moments to remember the last time you were relaxed and how good it felt.

When you are comfortable, take a nice, deep breath. Notice how the air fills your body.

> As you breathe out, let peaceful feelings move throughout your body.
>
> Let the rhythm of music calm you.
>
> Feel your muscles relax and your heartbeat and breathing slow.
>
> Say to yourself: "I am calm and relaxed."
>
> Take three slow breaths and each time you breathe out, relax all your muscles.

With your imagination, think about a large aquarium. Pretend that you, and all the other people who are in the waiting room, are actually beautiful tropical fish swimming in this large fish tank. Imagine that the clothes the people are wearing are actually their colorful scales. Take a few moments to make a picture in your mind of this large fish tank. Does your tank have some green plants in it? Does it have shells and colorful stones covering the bottom of it? Are there any little buildings in it?

Notice that there are many different types of fish in your aquarium and they all glide back and forth going their own way. Some of the fish have long tails that sway gently as they swim along. Other fish are tiny and they dart quickly around the plants.

Pretend that you can magically breathe underwater in your aquarium. Take a breath and then breathe out. As you let out your breath, you make air bubbles. Watch the bubbles float away above you. Your bubbles float up and join the bubbles from the other fish in the aquarium. You smile as you imagine all the breath bubbles floating above the heads of everyone you pass. Deep, slow breathing, in and out, calms you. Your heartbeat is calm and your stomach feels calm as you swim in the imaginary water.

Move around in the aquarium. Swim over to a patch of green seaweed. Hide in the grass for awhile and look around at all the other fish people. Big fish, little fish. Each one is beautiful in the water.

Some are rushing past. Some move slowly. Some are sitting quietly and watching the others. Some are talking to each other. You might see some who are sick and others with injuries. Each one is different and is here for a different reason.

You are happy to have some extra time to observe the gentle movement of people around you. You are all together in the same room, yet each of you is going his or her own way. Say to yourself three times: **"My day is filled with interesting people."**

When you are ready to return to the room, take a deep breath, and as you breathe out, open your eyes. You feel relaxed about being in the waiting room today. You are there for an important reason. You know that people are in waiting rooms for all different reasons. Using your imagination to think about interesting things helps the waiting time pass quickly and helps you feel calm.

Ship Deck

"I feel confident and calm in new experiences and new places."

Coaching Notes: *A visit to a hospital may be a new experience where you encounter new sights, sounds, and smells. You may wonder what brings all the people to the hospital. On your trip to the hospital, you can use your imagination to create a story about taking a voyage on an ocean liner.*

> **Take time to relax your muscles and take calm, peaceful breaths.** Use the following paragraph or another of your choice.
>
> Close your eyes gently, or focus on a picture or a spot near you.
>
> Take a few moments to remember the last time you were relaxed and how good it felt.
>
> When you are comfortable, take a nice, deep breath. Notice how the air fills your body.
>
> As you breathe out, let peaceful feelings move throughout your body.
>
> Let the rhythm of music calm you.

Feel your muscles relax and your heartbeat and breathing slow.
Say to yourself: "I am calm and relaxed."
Take three slow breaths and each time you breathe out, relax all your muscles.

I magine that an ocean voyage adventure is about to begin. You have boarded a large ocean liner and you feel a nervous, excited feeling in your stomach. This is the first time you have ever been on such a big boat. You begin to walk around and explore your new surroundings.

As you walk along the deck of the big ship, imagine holding onto the railing and looking into the water as the waves splash against the side of the ship. Look across the ocean and watch the dolphins jump out of the water and then dive back in. They seem to be guiding your ship. Notice the way the saltwater and seaweed swirl together. There is much to see on this voyage.

Take several gentle breaths and smell the breeze, filled with the scents of the ocean. Smell the fresh, salty ocean air. Listen to the seagulls caw above you. They are calling to you and saying, "Welcome. You will have a wonderful journey."

Feel the gentle motion of the ship as it moves along the waves. You can feel the motion of the ship throughout your whole body, and you sway as you walk along the deck. The feeling of the waves in your body feels like gentle rocking. It is a calm, peaceful feeling.

As the trip gets underway, walk over to a comfortable deck chair. Sit down and rest your head against the back of the chair. As you are relaxing, many people walk past you, each going his or her own way. Some of them smile at you and say hello. You say hello to them with a smile on your face. You are traveling with friendly people.

Say to yourself: **"I feel confident and calm in new experiences and new places."** You are seeing new faces, hearing new sounds, and smelling new fragrances. You are curious about all these new things and you look forward to seeing what will happen next.

Listen to the music of the waves, the wind, and the birds. You feel very peaceful on this part of your journey. You are rocking gently, and a calm feeling fills your body.

Keep this picture in your mind, and use your imagination to pretend you are on the ship whenever you are in the waiting room at the hospital or doctor's office. When you are in the waiting room, seated comfortably in a chair, pretend that you are in a deck chair on a ship. Use the sounds and smells around you to help picture yourself sailing over the ocean waves. Bring your story right into the waiting room with you.

Imagine that your nurses and doctors are with you on this voyage. They make you as comfortable as possible as you wait for your appointment. Take slow breaths in and then breathe out gently. The rhythm of your breathing helps you feel relaxed. This feeling stays with you during your visit to the hospital or doctor's office. Repeat to yourself: **"I feel confident and calm in new experiences and new places."**

Look around. There are other people in the waiting room. Pretend all the people you see are taking an exciting trip on a boat. Make up stories about where the people are going.

When you are ready to return to the room, take a deep breath. As you breathe out, open your eyes. You feel refreshed and relaxed. You are able to be calm before and during your visits to your doctor and the hospital when you use your imagination. You are able to rest quietly during a new procedure because you think about being on a new adventure on a ship. The next time you are waiting, tell your coach about the stories you are imagining. It makes the waiting time go quickly and it helps you feel calm and relaxed in new places.

116

BLAST-OFF!

"My stomach stays calm and steady."

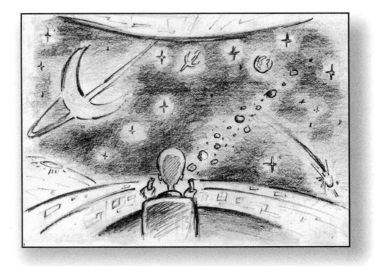

Coaching Notes: *Sometimes stomachs feel queasy on the trip to a medical appointment even before reaching the hospital or doctor's office. In this story, you pretend to get ready for your appointment the way an astronaut gets ready for a launch. You can think about this story as you travel to your own appointments. The images in this story may be especially helpful before a chemotherapy treatment.*

Take time to relax your muscles and take calm, peaceful breaths. Use the following paragraph or another of your choice.

Close your eyes gently, or focus on a picture or a spot near you.

Take a few moments to remember the last time you were relaxed and how good it felt.

When you are comfortable, take a nice, deep breath. Notice how the air fills your body.

As you breathe out, let peaceful feelings move throughout your body.

Let the rhythm of music calm you.

> Feel your muscles relax and your heartbeat and breathing slow.
> Say to yourself: "I am calm and relaxed."
> Take three slow breaths and each time you breathe out, relax all your muscles.

Imagine that you are an astronaut getting ready for a launch into outer space. Picture yourself leaving home and traveling to the launch pad in a specially designed bus with other astronauts. As you drive to the space center, think about the things you will need for your upcoming trip into outer space. You need special gear. You need a spacesuit with tubing connected to it. You need a special chair to sit in during the flight. The flight crew is getting all these things ready for you.

Your bus reaches the launch pad, and as you walk to the spaceship, many people wave to you and say hello. They are the people in Mission Control who will work with you to make sure you have a successful trip. Wave, smile, and let them know you are ready when they are.

When an astronaut reaches the launch pad, you would think the astronaut could just sit back and relax, but the astronaut must be prepared for many feelings at launch time. Now it is almost your turn. No one can tell by looking at you, but your stomach already feels like it blasted off! It is rocking and rolling inside of you. Sometimes thinking about something ahead of time fills you with nervous or excited feelings. That is why you feel the way you do even before getting into the spaceship.

Now, imagine walking up the ramp that leads into your spaceship. When you enter, take a look around at the shiny buttons and lights in the cabin. As you settle in for your flight, check all your equipment. Make sure the tubing is connected to your spacesuit. Adjust your chair to a comfortable position for your flight. Talk to the crew and let them know you are ready.

"You are now cleared for take-off! All systems go!" These are words you hear before your spaceship blasts off. The message lets you know that everything is ready. Everything is safe. Now listen to the countdown and notice that you become more relaxed with the sound of each number. Ten–nine–eight–seven–six–five–four–three –two–one–Blast Off!

With a whoosh, the feeling in your body changes as you begin the journey. It feels like being in a roller coaster rushing through the air. Breathe slowly and calmly as your body makes the adjustments to outer space.

You enter an asteroid field and the space rocks crash around you. The spaceship lurches from the impact of the asteroids. You are the commander of the ship and you are at the controls. You make a decision to go into hyperdrive, which zooms you away from the asteroids and all other disturbances. You are able to steady your ship.

Right away, you feel the difference. The ship travels with a smooth feeling. And now there is a smooth feeling in your stomach and head. Say to yourself: **"My stomach stays calm and steady."** There is no worry or tightness anywhere in your body.

Now you can enjoy the ride. This is the best part. Relax in your chair and take a deep breath. Now, breathe out any bumpiness that you were feeling in your body. Breathe in peacefulness. Repeat to yourself three times: **"My stomach stays calm and steady."** Continue your calm, steady breathing throughout your trip.

Remember that you are the captain and you can choose to stay on a smooth path. Take some time to imagine looking through the spaceship window to see the spectacular sights outside. When you land, you will remember the calm, peaceful feelings of this trip and the beauty of outer space.

When you are ready to come back to your room take a deep breath. As you breathe out, open your eyes and drift back feeling relaxed and calm. On your next trip to your doctor's office or to the hospital for treatment, think about getting ready for a trip into outer space and count down to a smooth take-off. Slow, gentle breathing, and making pictures in your mind helps you stay on a calming course. You can look at interesting things and do activities that are fun as you wait for your appointments and as you have treatments.

PEACEFUL SWAMP

"I am comfortable, as I lie quiet and still."

Coaching Notes: *This is a story to help you lie quiet and still during your diagnostic scans or radiation treatments. During tests or radiation treatments, you can use your imagination and pretend to be a peaceful alligator. Think about your quiet, peaceful body lying on the treatment or radiation table, just as an alligator lies quietly in a swamp.*

Take time to relax your muscles and take calm, peaceful breaths. Use the following paragraph or another of your choice.

Close your eyes gently, or focus on a picture or a spot near you.

Take a few moments to remember the last time you were relaxed and how good it felt.

When you are comfortable, take a nice, deep breath. Notice how the air fills your body.

As you breathe out, let peaceful feelings move throughout your body.

Let the rhythm of music calm you.

Feel your muscles relax and your heartbeat and breathing slow.

Say to yourself: "I am calm and relaxed."

Take three slow breaths and each time you breathe out, relax all your muscles.

On a visit to a swamp, the first thing you notice is the quiet peacefulness. The calm air feels heavy and humid. Reeds and vines grow along the edges of the water. Shades of green surround you and provide camouflage for the residents of the swamp. Look around carefully. Who lives here?

Occasionally, a small bird takes flight and lands a short distance away on the branch of a tree. You spot a snake as it silently slithers through the cattails. Listen to the croak of a distant frog as it cuts the silence hanging over the swamp. Dragonflies with beautiful, green wings flit back and forth in front of you. Relax, and breathe gently on your visit to this beautiful place.

In your imagination, listen to all of the different sounds that you can hear in the swamp. The songs of the birds, the chirping of insects, the buzzing of cicadas are like soft music that you might hear.

The swamp is also the home of crocodiles and alligators. They live peacefully with the other animals in this swamp. They rest under the water. Only their noses poke out of the water. They are as still as logs. Crocodiles and alligators can be very still for a long time. They are protected by their stillness and camouflage coloring. Even a person in a canoe paddling slowly past will not notice them.

When you have a scan, diagnostic procedure, or treatment, use your imagination to pretend that you are one of the peaceful alligators in this swamp. When you are asked to lie on the treatment table, pretend you are in the calm, quiet swamp. Make a picture in your mind of being as relaxed and still as an alligator. You lie still and comfortable just the way an alligator lies on a rock. You are safe and you have no worries because everything is peaceful in your swamp.

As you breathe quietly, say to yourself: **"I am comfortable, as I lie quiet and still."** This helps you feel relaxed during the minutes that you have your test or treatment.

When your treatment begins, you may hear the machine make a buzzing sound. It buzzes like an insect close to your ear. Imagine it is like the sound of a bug or bird that an alligator might hear in a swamp.

When you see the large radiation machine or scanner come close to your body, pretend that it is a canoe slipping through your swamp. Imagine that you are able to lie so still that the person paddling the canoe does not even spot you.

Your body is relaxed and resting — just the way an alligator rests in shallow water. Listen to the noises around you. Let your thoughts drift to a swamp and pretend to be a peaceful alligator resting quietly on a rock. Repeat to yourself three times: **"I am comfortable, as I lie quiet and still."**

When you are ready to come back to the room, take a deep breath. As you breathe out, open your eyes. You feel relaxed and calm. Your treatment is over for the day. The technician will help you get off the treatment table. You can stretch and sit up.

The time flew by because you used your imagination to think about being still and relaxed. At times when you need to stay in one position, you can remember being an alligator on your visit to the quiet swamp.

THINKING ABOUT DIAGNOSTIC MEDICAL TESTS

Tips from Derek, who was treated for kidney disease and received a kidney transplant

It was important that my family always told me what was going on and that they told me the truth about what was going to happen. It was also good to know my family was always there with me.

Some of the things our doctors need to know about our health cannot be seen or felt from the outside. Luckily, our doctors can choose from a wide assortment of medical tests to find out what is happening inside our bodies. Some of the tests described below may be ordered for you.

Maybe you've wished you had x-ray vision so you could see inside a present before you opened it up. It would be fun to be able to see the insides of things. Doctors are able to look inside our bodies using **x-rays**, and **CT scans** (computerized axial tomography), and **MRIs** (magnetic resonance imaging), and **ultrasound.**

These types of x-ray pictures and scans help doctors look at the inside of a person's body to get information about organs such as the lungs, liver, and stomach. Some scans can also examine our brain and bones. If a person is having a brain scan, the scanner cannot tell what the person is thinking. It can only take a special picture of the parts of the brain.

All of the tests are done to help make a diagnosis or to see how well treatment is working. A diagnosis is a doctor's opinion of what is causing a patient's problem. Test results are important in making a good diagnosis and so is the information a patient tells a doctor.

What You Can Expect

All four methods use machines that are usually found in special rooms at the medical center or hospital. The machines are big and will be interesting for you to look at. Technicians who are trained to operate them will explain what you need to do during the test. They will let you know what to expect. This information will help you feel comfortable.

Before some of the procedures, you may need a shot that helps the pictures show up more clearly on x-ray film. One type of injection uses a "contrast dye." This type of dye helps us see parts of your body better. Don't be confused by the other word "die." The words sound alike, but they mean very different things.

Another type uses a radioactive substance. The substance will collect in certain places in your body and then the doctor will use a machine that measures radioactivity to learn about the part of the body being examined. The nurse or doctor will explain any sensations that you may feel in your body from the injection.

None of the machines will cause any painful surprises or pokes while you are being examined. Some of them will make noises. You may wish to ask what kinds of sounds, smells, or other feelings to expect during the test. You may ask as many questions as you like.

Resting Quietly and Staying Comfortable

When you are having your picture taken at home, you have to stand still so the picture is not blurry. It is the same with the scanners at the hospital. You have to keep your body in one position while the scans are being taken.

You can help yourself lie quietly by using your peaceful breathing and by thinking about stories that help you become relaxed. The nurses will also help you. Nurses have medicine available that a child can take before a procedure. The medication helps a child become prepared and comfortable during tests.

You might be given medicine called an anesthetic to make you unconscious or to numb painful sensations. One type of anesthetic is Emla™ cream that numbs a small part of your skin if you are getting an injection or needle stick. Another type of anesthetic is called sedation medicine and it treats your whole body and makes you unaware of discomfort.

Tiny Cells Tell a Big Story

Each part of your body is made up of many different types of cells and they all have different jobs to do. For example, we have lung cells to help us breathe, and muscle cells to help us move, and brain cells to help us think. A cell is the basic unit of all living things. Examining cells from the inside of your body is another way for doctors to gain information.

Our bodies are made up of trillions of cells so if a doctor needs a small sample of cells they can be removed from inside your body and your body quickly makes new ones to replace them. A doctor removes cells from the body by doing a biopsy, a bone marrow aspiration, or a lumbar puncture (also called a spinal tap or LP.)

Cells are very tiny and you can only see them by looking through a microscope. A doctor, called a pathologist, will look at your cells to see if any changes have taken place. The pathologist will report to your doctor, and your doctor will use that information to give you the best possible treatment.

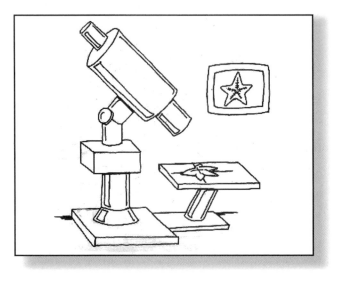

Inside Information

In addition to doing scans and biopsies, your doctors gain information from your blood and urine. You may be asked to give a blood or urine sample to a medical technologist who studies it and reports to your doctor. Each time these samples are tested, the doctor compares the results to tests done earlier and is able to record your progress. Your doctor only orders tests as often as needed to get information about your health.

When a blood sample is taken, it is done carefully by taking some blood out of a vein or by a finger stick. When this is done, you may feel a poke. You might notice a little red spot on your skin from the needle. Your skin closes up the spot right away so the blood does not leak. You may be given a bandage or piece of gauze to cover the spot. No matter how much blood is taken, you won't run out. Your body is always busy making more blood.

127

Some children have a catheter, called a central line. The catheter can be used for giving medicine and for taking blood tests. When it is used for blood tests there is no poking sensation.

DOCTORS GET INFORMATION IN MANY WAYS

Here are descriptions of some of the tests that children might have that give important information to their health care team. Ask your doctor or nurse if there are any others that might be used in your care.

Biopsy: Cells are removed from the body and examined under a microscope to see if there are any signs of disease in the tissue (cells) that was removed. Usually a local anesthetic is all that is needed to make a person comfortable but sometimes, general anesthesia may be used depending on the location of the tissue to be removed.

Blood Studies: Blood may be taken from a vein with a syringe, by a finger stick, or through a catheter. A sample of blood cells is taken to check the number of white cells, red cells and platelets in the blood. A **CBC (Complete Blood Count)**, examines the components of blood. The tests help diagnose certain health problems and follow the results of treatment.

Bone Marrow Aspiration: Bone marrow is the soft tissue in the hollow of long bones where red blood cells and other types of cells are made. The doctor may take a small sample of bone marrow from one of the bones in the chest, hip, spine or leg to determine the condition of the marrow and whether or not cancer cells are present. The procedure lasts five to ten minutes. The patient may be helped to relax by using a short acting sedation medication or a local anesthetic to numb the skin.

Computerized Axial Tomography: A CAT or CT scan is a specialized x-ray machine that can detect differences in the way x-rays are absorbed in different tissues. The body tissues can be examined for masses or other changes. The patient is asked to lie still on a table while the x-ray beam rotates around the person's body. The table slides in and out of a machine that goes all the way around your body. Some people think the machine's round hole looks like a really big donut hole.

Electrocardiogram (ECG/EKG): This is a machine that tests the health of your heart. Small pieces of rubber, which are attached by wires to the machine, are taped to various places on your body. The machine records your heart's rhythm and the force of each heartbeat. The test does not cause any discomfort.

Lumbar Puncture: This procedure is also called a **spinal tap or LP.** The technique removes a small amount of the fluid that surrounds the brain and spinal cord. The fluid is examined for cancer cells and other material. The patient is asked to lie on his or her side and curl the body into a ball. The patient may be helped to relax by using a short acting sedation medication. A local anesthetic is used to numb an area on your back and then a needle is inserted into the fluid space between the vertebrae and the spinal cord. The needle does not injure the spinal cord. The test takes five or ten minutes. You may be asked to lie still on your back for an hour or more after this test. This helps to avoid a headache that might be a side effect of the test. This procedure may also be used to administer medicine directly to the brain or spinal cord.

Scans: A scan takes a picture that shows the inside of the body such as the liver, brain or bones. A radioactive chemical is swallowed or injected prior to the scan and given time to travel through the body. A special camera called a scanner detects the radioactivity and takes pictures. Doctors are able to tell whether or not the organs are working correctly and whether or not they contain abnormal masses or tumors. During the scan the patient is asked to lie still on a table as a machine passes around the body.

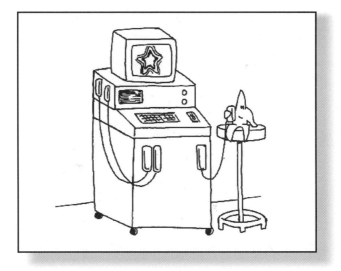

Ultrasound Studies: Ultrasounds make pictures through the use of sound waves that bounce off organs and other internal structures. Sound waves, above the frequency that can be heard by the human ear, create echo patterns. The sound waves can be changed electronically into images that are then changed into pictures. Different types of tissues generate different echoes and a doctor can make a diagnosis from the image. The patient lies on a table and a small instrument (it looks like the paddle from an air hockey game) emits sound waves as it is slowly moved over the part of the body that the doctor wants to see. A clear gel is put on the paddle so it will move slowly and evenly over the skin. The gel may feel cool on the skin.

X-Rays: This is a test using low doses of radiation that can be used to examine specific body parts to diagnose diseases. The patient is asked to be still for the brief time, (about five seconds), that is needed to take the picture.

Getting Ready for a Test

The first time you have any medical procedure you may feel nervous and unsure about what to expect. You can practice feeling calm and relaxed when you experience any medical procedure. This will make the moments easier for you. With a little practice, you will become very good at helping yourself feel peaceful - even in a noisy, busy hospital.

Taking deep breaths, making pictures in your mind, and creating stories are all helpful ways to stay calm and relaxed. You can bring favorite books, tapes, and CDs with you. A stuffed toy or special blanket is terrific for hugging. Coloring pictures as you wait helps time go quickly. You and your coach will be able to think of just the right thing to bring with you. Each diagnostic procedure provides valuable information. You want your doctor to have the best information possible about your health, so your job is to make yourself comfortable throughout each test and appointment. In addition to the things you can do to help yourself feel comfortable, your nurses also know ways to help you.

Once you start a treatment plan, one of your big questions might be whether the plan is working. Are you getting healthier? If the sickness is inside the body the way to tell is to look inside your body, or test body fluids, or examine cells. You can expect to have more of the same tests and, when you do, you will think of ways to help yourself feel calm and brave.

STORIES FOR HELPING WITH PAINFUL SENSATIONS

Tips from Jon, who was treated for leukemia

When I had to get a shot in my legs, I would wiggle my toes and it wouldn't hurt as much.

Ouch! That hurts! Think of the last time that you said those words. What was it that made you hurt? Sometimes things hurt us and we give a little shout or even shed a few tears. Most times, we are surprised when we feel an ache. We didn't expect it to happen. We stub a toe, fall on the ground, or pinch a finger: *Yowie!* How did that happen?

Other times, the painful feeling lasts longer, like when we have a headache, or sprain an ankle, or have a sore throat. When we think pain is going to stick around for awhile, we might take pain medicine to help control the discomfort.

There are other things we do to help ourselves when something hurts. How about the hug and kiss you get to make you feel better? Think about a time that you used an ice pack on a bump to make the hurt go away. Have you ever tried to do a new activity, like play a game or read a book, so you wouldn't think about the discomfort anymore? All of those things work. You can use them when you want to help yourself feel less pain or feel less nervous.

Pain is a Message

First, let's think about why we feel pain. Pain is a message. All parts of your body send out messages to your brain through your nerve cells. Your nerve cells are attached to your spinal cord. The messages go back and forth from your brain to smaller nerves everywhere in your body.

If you think of the trunk of a tree growing to smaller and then still smaller branches, you have an image of your spinal cord going from a "trunk" to smaller, then still smaller nerves. Your brain can take in messages and send them out at the same time. In that way, you react quickly when something is wrong somewhere in your body and you can try to change whatever it is that is causing pain.

Sometimes, pain sticks around for a long time, and maybe we are not even exactly sure what is causing the problem. Unfortunately, when you are sick, there is a certain amount of pain that you can't avoid, but your parents and those who take care of you will help you. It is important to know that you do not have to worry about pain.

Being able to describe the way you feel is important. Sometimes a nervous feeling might feel like a "knot in your stomach" or "butterflies in your stomach." Sometimes painful feelings are like a "sharp nail" or a "stinging bee."

There are many ways to describe pain. Think about words that you could use to tell someone how you feel. It helps to figure out a way to talk about pain and to let others know when it started, how long it has lasted, if the ache is big or small, if it happens when you move a certain way, if it comes and goes, or if you feel it all the time.

Rating Pain

Another way to describe pain is to figure out a way to tell "how much" it hurts. A helpful way to tell someone how much pain you are feeling is to rate it on a scale of zero to five. The number zero would mean you are not feeling any painful sensations. At the other end of the number line, a five would mean you are feeling lots of discomfort. The numbers in between gradually increase from zero to five in the amount of pain you feel.

Talk about things that have felt painful to you in the past and tell your coach where they would fit on the line between zero and five. Now you can describe new sensations by comparing them to other feelings on the number line.

The starfish faces on this number line show how things might feel to you on the rating scale. Starfish # 5 has tears coming out of its eyes, but you do not need to be crying to be feeling lots of pain.

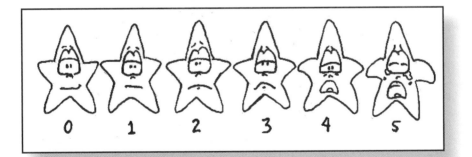

Share Your Feelings

Always tell someone if you feel worried or nervous about something hurting. You should always talk to an adult if you have pain so a plan can be started to help you. Doctors understand pain and have many ways to treat it. There is not one best or only way to treat pain so you might use a few different methods.

Helpful Stories

The next stories can be used when you want to concentrate on having good feelings in your body. There are going to be things in our lives that hurt. It might be for a few seconds or it could last for awhile. If you know ahead of time that something might hurt, you can use a story with positive statements and calm breathing to prepare yourself to be relaxed. You can use a story, positive statements, and calm breathing to interrupt the painful message and give your body a different message on which to concentrate.

These stories can help you feel more comfortable: **"Paintbrush," "Hot Air Balloon," "The Slide," "Dolphins," "Field of Flowers," "Candles,"** and **"A Flag."**

Reread the **"Progressive Muscle Relaxation"** scripts for more help with feeling comfortable.

PAINTBRUSH

"I can brush away pain."

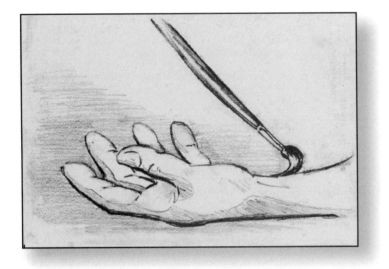

Coaching Notes: *Your skin is made up of billions of cells. You send messages to your brain through your skin cells. In this story, you can use a real paintbrush to stimulate the skin as a way to distract yourself from uncomfortable sensations in your body. The bristles of your brush should have enough firmness for you to feel a slight tickle when you brush them over your skin. You can use the paintbrush by yourself or you can ask your coach to brush your skin while you concentrate on feeling comfortable. If a paintbrush is not available, use your fingertips or a textured fabric. Adapt the story for the approach that you are using. This story may be especially helpful to feel calm while you wait for medication to take effect.*

Take time to relax your muscles and take calm, peaceful breaths.
Use the following paragraph or another of your choice.

Close your eyes gently, or focus on a picture or a spot near you.

Take a few moments to remember the last time you were relaxed and how good it felt.

> When you are comfortable, take a nice, deep breath. Notice how the air fills your body.
>
> As you breathe out, let peaceful feelings move throughout your body.
>
> Let the rhythm of music calm you. Feel your muscles relax and your heartbeat and breathing slow.
>
> Say to yourself: "I am calm and relaxed."
>
> Take three slow breaths and each time you breathe out, relax all your muscles.

Use your imagination to think about one of your favorite colors. Is it a sunny yellow color? Maybe it is a peachy-orange like the color of delicious fruit. Is it green like the color of leaves on the trees in spring? Now, imagine a room filled with cans of paint of all different colors. Out of all those colors, choose the pot of paint filled with a light shade of your favorite color. Open the lid and look inside the pot. Yes, it's just right. Maybe the color you chose matches your skin so perfectly that it couldn't even be seen if you dipped your finger into the pot. That would be a great color for brushing onto your skin.

Now, dip your brush into the can of paint. Swirl the tip of your brush in the perfect color. Pull the brush out of the pot and gently tap it on the rim. Let the extra drips fall back into the can. You are ready to do some very special painting. Choose a little patch of your skin and brush the imaginary paint onto that spot.

Brush your skin in a gentle rhythm, back and forth. Take a few moments to enjoy this gentle back-and-forth motion on your skin. As you brush your skin, imagine that you are sending a message to your body with your paintbrush. Say to yourself: **"I can brush away pain."**

When you brush your skin, you will brush away uncomfortable feelings and pain. Breathe in and out with the rhythm of your paintbrush. Brush on coolness and comfort.

The motion of the brush makes tickling sensations on your skin.

As you focus on those feelings you do not notice other sensations else-where in your body. Gentle brushing, back and forth. Concentrate on the gentle movements on your skin that are brushing away discom-fort.

Now, use your imagination and your special paintbrush to add more comfort to your body. Imagine dipping your brush into another pot filled with a special, magical paint. This incredible paint makes your skin feel numb when it touches it. When it goes on your skin, the pain goes away.

Go to the part of your body that feels uncomfortable. Brush the paint back and forth on your skin. Move the brush gently back and forth, imagining that you are painting a numbing medicine onto your body. Brush away the tenderness. Your special paint covers the uncomfortable place with a beautiful color.

The numb feeling sinks through your skin into your body. Does it feel warm or cool as it sinks into the sore spot? Does it sink quickly, or does it glide slowly to the spot? Use your breathing to blow the numbing paint wherever you want it to go inside your body.

Your wonderful, beautiful, paint is working. Now you feel more comfortable. The comfortable feeling stays with you even after you stop brushing your skin. Repeat to yourself three times: **"I can brush away pain."** Your magic paint and magic paintbrush are always ready for you. They are in your imagination, and you can take them wher-ever you want to go.

When you are ready to return to your room, take a deep breath. As you breathe out, open your eyes and notice that you feel refreshed and relaxed. Use your magic paintbrush at times when you would like to brush on comfort and brush away pain.

HOT AIR BALLOON

"My body feels comfortable and at peace."

Coaching Notes: *In this story, a ride in a hot air balloon encourages you to rise above sensations of pain or discomfort. You will take an imaginary trip in your very own hot air balloon and you will think about being high above any problems or worries. Uncomfortable feelings will sink away.*

A hot air balloon travels on air currents like a feather floating on the wind, or an eagle soaring through the sky. A burner is attached to the balloon and it heats up the air inside the balloon. The pilot makes the balloon go up and down by controlling the temperature of the air.

> **Take time to relax your muscles and take calm, peaceful breaths.**
> Use the following paragraph or another of your choice.
> Close your eyes gently, or focus on a picture or a spot near you.

Take a few moments to remember the last time you were relaxed and how good it felt. When you are comfortable, take a nice, deep breath. Notice how the air fills your body.

As you breathe out, let peaceful feelings move throughout your body.

Let the rhythm of music calm you. Feel your muscles relax and your heartbeat and breathing slow.

Say to yourself: "I am calm and relaxed."

Take three slow breaths and each time you breathe out, relax all your muscles.

Make a picture in your mind of a hot air balloon; your very own balloon. Choose your favorite colors to make a design on it. Let your imagination go wild. Is your balloon in the shape of one of your favorite animals? Maybe it has words printed on it; words that describe how you feel today. Think about decorating the huge balloon with pictures of things that are very special to you. Imagine seeing your drawings expand in the sky as your balloon fills up with air.

Next, attach a basket for passengers. Attach the basket to your balloon with strong ropes.

Listen to the whooshing sound as the burners heat the air inside your balloon. The sound lets you know that you are almost ready to take off.

Your trip has an important mission. Your mission is to travel away from feelings that make you mad, or sad, or worried, or uncomfortable. Imagine that you can pack up all of those unwanted feelings. It's a funny thought, and it makes you smile to imagine packing up those feelings. Put them into a suitcase and close it tightly. What does the suitcase look like to you? Does it have a strong lock? Is it big or small? Leave the suitcase on the ground beside the basket. The suitcase will not be part of this trip. You will travel in comfort. Your unwanted feelings will stay behind.

Now you are ready. Climb into the basket. You may invite others to go with you. Once you are in the basket, it is time to begin your trip. Your trip will last as long as you choose. Your heart is pounding with excitement as the balloon lifts off and begins to rise above the ground. You feel light as you lift off.

As the balloon rises, feel the rush of fresh air surround your body. Let the breeze smooth out the muscles on your face. Your forehead, cheeks, and chin are relaxed.

Take a breath and let the fresh air fill your lungs. As you breathe out, make a sound like the whooshing sound of the burners or a candle being blown out.

Look down at the land below. Hooray! You can see the old suitcase getting tinier, and tinier, and sinking into the ground! Those heavy, unwanted feelings are gone. What a relief! Are there any other unwanted feelings that you want to toss overboard? Imagine dumping any leftover pain, or sadness, or anger, or worry over the side of the basket. Watch as those feelings fall away from you and also sink into the ground.

The feeling of lightness fills your body. Let your muscles release all heaviness and tightness. Relax as the feelings of lightness and peacefulness fill your body. There is no room for uncomfortable feelings in a body that is filled with lightness. As your body relaxes, continue breathing slowly and gently. With each slow breath, let the color of the sky fill you.

The higher you go, the smaller things look on the ground. The sounds from below fade away. You are surrounded by the sound of the wind as you travel gently on the air currents. It is a new adventure for you, a new way of seeing the world.

Breathe in happiness. Breathe out feelings of sadness. Say to yourself: **"My body feels comfortable and at peace."** Let this feeling drift through your body. Repeat, **"My body feels comfortable and at peace."** Each breath fills you with a color that feels peaceful to you.

Each breath carries you gently, softly through the blue sky.

If you choose to, you can look down at the ground. Describe the colors and the sizes of the things you observe. You might notice the shadows that your balloon makes on the ground below you as you travel through the sky. People and cars might look like tiny ants as you imagine them moving along the streets. The suitcase of unwanted feelings that you left behind on the ground is nowhere to be seen. Repeat again, **"My body feels comfortable and at peace."**

When you have traveled as far as you would like to go, and you are ready to return, you can bring the balloon slowly down to the ground. Your breath moves the balloon along. With the whooshing sound of air blowing out of your lips, you land in just the right place; the place you started from, but with a very important difference. The suitcase you left behind is gone.

Drift gently back to the room feeling refreshed and relaxed. Take a deep breath and as you breathe out, open your eyes. You feel calm and relaxed after your imaginary journey.

If you notice any unwanted feelings returning, it is easy for you to go up and away from them again. You can fly higher and be more comfortable, just as you did before, by using your breath and concentrating on the pictures in your mind. Whenever you want to be more comfortable you can remember your hot air balloon trip. You rise above discomfort because you make yourself feel light and you calm your body with positive messages.

THE SLIDE

"I climb up to good feelings."

Coaching Notes: *You can use this story to feel more comfortable and to rise above painful sensations.*

Take time to relax your muscles and take calm, peaceful breaths. Use the following paragraph or another of your choice.

Close your eyes gently, or focus on a picture or a spot near you.

Take a few moments to remember the last time you were relaxed and how good it felt. When you are comfortable, take a nice, deep breath. Notice how the air fills your body.

143

As you breathe out, let peaceful feelings move throughout your body. Let the rhythm of music calm you. Feel your muscles relax and your heartbeat and breathing slow.

Say to yourself: "I am calm and relaxed."

Take three slow breaths and each time you breathe out, relax all your muscles.

Make a picture in your mind of an enormous playground. Imagine that it has all of your favorite equipment on it. There is a wonderful, tall slide in the center. Look around. There are no other children at the playground! You have the slide all to yourself.

Just as you are about to start climbing up the wide steps, you notice a small sign that says, *"If you want to use the slide you must leave something at the bottom."* You think that is an interesting idea, and you wonder for a moment what you could leave behind.

Aha! You think of a great idea. You decide to leave behind any heavy, hurting feelings that are inside your body. You do not want to lift the heaviness of any pain up the ladder. Luckily, you find a sack lying on the ground at the bottom of the steps. Open the sack. Put all your unwanted feelings in it. Close up the sack and leave the feelings of pain behind! Now you are ready to take the first step.

Put your hands on the railings and start to climb. Take a gentle breath and as you breathe out, climb up the first step, then the second step. With each step, your body relaxes more and more. Notice your body lift away from the sensations that made you feel uncomfortable. Climb up the third, then fourth, then fifth step with more relaxation and slow, calm breathing at every step. Climb slowly.

The higher you go on the steps, the farther away you are from any pain, and the more comfortable you feel. You rise above any discomfort. Say to yourself: **"I climb up to good feelings."** Continue climbing.

With your next breath, you reach the top step. Now you can sit on top of the slide feeling happy and relaxed. Say to yourself: **"I climb up to good feelings."**

You are as high as the clouds. Take a deep breath and as you breathe out, blow the feathery clouds away. Put your lips together and concentrate on blowing away a wisp of a cloud. Watch it change shape as you blow it away. You are filled with comfortable feelings from your head to your toes as you blow away the clouds.

Your head reaches up into the blue sky and the sun warms and relaxes your body. Focus on the wonderful feeling of the sun shining on you. As you breathe, feel the air fill your lungs with healing strength. The air expands into every cell in your body and brings calmness, comfort and healing.

The golden light of the sun reaches the ground and melts away the sack you left behind. The heavy, hurting sensations are melting away. They are draining away into the ground. The unwanted feelings are gone.

Make pictures in your mind of this playground and your view from this tall slide. The pictures will stay in your memory and you will be able to remember them any time you want to help yourself feel comfortable.

When you feel ready, give yourself a small push and glide down the long slide. A cool breeze touches your face as you go down the slide. You feel light and peaceful.

When you reach the bottom of the slide, a magic carpet catches you. As you rest on the carpet, you can make a choice. If you are comfortable with the way you feel, you can imagine the magic carpet taking you to any place on the playground to play. Or, if you would like to rise above any uncomfortable feelings, the carpet can take you back to the bottom of the ladder so you can climb up again and continue to focus on your breathing and on feeling light.

Repeat again with your inner voice, **"I climb up to good feelings."**

When you feel comfortable and are ready to leave the playground and the slide, take a breath and open your eyes. As you breathe out, return to the room feeling refreshed. The warm, light, comfortable feeling stays with you.

145

DOLPHINS

"I can go to a calm, pain free place."

Coaching Notes: *Previous stories used the image of rising to sunshine to ease discomfort. Sometimes an opposite image works better. For example, a severe headache or fever may make a person want to find a dim, cool, quiet spot. In this story, a dolphin will guide you through cool water to help you find a place to relax.*

The images in this story may help you prepare for anesthesia, or for procedures requiring sedation.

Dolphins are friendly mammals who live in the ocean. Dolphins have a way to communicate with each other by using clicking noises. People have studied dolphins and learned about the sounds they make. Dolphins can be taught to understand commands from the people who train them. There are stories about dolphins swimming through the ocean to find people who are in need of help.

Take time to relax your muscles and take calm, peaceful breaths. Use the following paragraph or another of your choice.

Close your eyes gently, or focus on a picture or a spot near you.

Take a few moments to remember the last time you were relaxed and how good it felt. When you are comfortable, take a nice, deep breath. Notice how the air fills your body.

As you breathe out, let peaceful feelings move throughout your body. Let the rhythm of music calm you. Feel your muscles relax and your heartbeat and breathing slow.

Say to yourself: "I am calm and relaxed."

Take three slow breaths and each time you breathe out, relax all your muscles.

Today you would like some help. You want to find a cool, quiet place to rest. You want to feel more comfortable. In your mind's eye, make a picture of yourself walking along a sandy beach at an ocean, looking for just the right place. As you walk along, what do you see? Do you picture a beach filled with seashells? Are there clumps of sea grass sticking up through the sand? Do bits of seaweed tickle the soles of your feet? Notice all the colors of the water and sand. Smell the salty air. Breathe gently, and enjoy your walk.

Now imagine walking along the shore until you find a cove, a small inlet, with calm water. It is very peaceful here. There are no noisy birds playing overhead and no jet skis zooming past. The only sound you hear is the gentle lapping of small waves.

The sky is cloudy today. The shady sky is perfect for you. The clouds block the sun so you do not have to squint. Let your eyes rest. Walk along the shore until your find a calm spot where you can wade into the ocean.

Now picture yourself slowly stepping into the gentle waves. First, your toes and knees feel cool. Then, as you go deeper, the water cools your arms and body. Gently bring some of the cool water to your face and head. You feel refreshed from the ocean water. Enjoy this feeling.

Now imagine going all the way into the water. You lean into the water and begin to swim. Pull your arms through the water and feel the rest of your body float. Glide in the coolness of the dark water. Pull with your arms. Kick with your legs, then glide through the water. It takes no effort to move through the water.

Your breathing is in rhythm with your arms and legs. Breathe, pull, and glide. With each pull of your arms, your head dips into the water. The movement calms you.

As you swim, a dolphin joins you and swims beside you. The dolphin is graceful in the water and so are you. Glide smoothly, with the dolphin by your side.

The dolphin talks to you. You discover that you can understand its clicking noises and the dolphin can understand your words. Tell the dolphin what hurts. Tell the dolphin that you need to feel more comfortable.

The dolphin understands you and swims gently by your side. You glide together on the surface and enjoy your movement in the comfortable water. As you swim together, the dolphin leads you to a rock with a scuba tank sitting on top of it. Imagine slipping the tank on your back and putting the breathing tube in your mouth. Now, you and the dolphin are able to dive.

You follow the dolphin as it dives deeper into the ocean. The dolphin guides you to a place where you are more comfortable. The dolphin leads you to a dimly lit, quiet place. Say to yourself: **"I can go to a calm, pain free place."**

Your dolphin leads you to a spot on smooth sand where you can curl up and rest. As you rest, you watch the seaweed sway gently around you. Fish swim by gracefully. The peaceful world below the surface of the water flows gently around you. Repeat again, **"I can go to a calm, pain free place."** You are calm and relaxed.

The dolphin glides up next to you and you feel its smooth skin. You tell the dolphin that you feel better and are ready to leave your comfortable spot. The dolphin lets you hold onto its fin and pulls you through the water. There is nothing sharp or rough near you. Everything is smooth and cool. Slide through the water and create gentle ripples behind you. Notice how good your body feels as you glide through the water. Enjoy your journey. Repeat again, **"I can go to a calm, pain free place."**

(Coaching Note: *If your child is resting comfortably and you do not want to disturb him or her you can eliminate the next paragraph.*)

When you are ready to return from your journey, take a deep breath. As you breathe out, open your eyes, and return to the room. Whenever you need to feel more comfortable, remember your journey with a dolphin in the cool, quiet waters of the ocean and know that you can use your imagination to take you to that place.

FIELD OF FLOWERS

"I am able to make myself feel comfortable."

Coaching Notes: *Sometimes part of you hurts and you feel pain. Sometimes you need a treatment or a medical test that is uncomfortable. You cannot avoid the treatment but you can change the way it feels to you. It is possible to lessen uncomfortable sensations by using yourimagination to focus on other feelings. In this story you will learn a way to change painful or uncomfortable feelings so they seem smaller to you.*

Take time to relax your muscles and take calm, peaceful breaths. Use the following paragraph or another of your choice.

Close your eyes gently, or focus on a picture or a spot near you.

Take a few moments to remember the last time you were relaxed and how good it felt. When you are comfortable, take a nice, deep breath. Notice how the air fills your body.

As you breathe out, let peaceful feelings move throughout your body. Let the rhythm of music calm you. Feel your muscles relax and your heartbeat and breathing slow.

> Say to yourself: "I am calm and relaxed."
> Take three slow breaths and each time you breathe out, relax all your muscles.

Imagine that you are sitting outside looking at a field of wild flowers. Gaze at the bright colors of the flowers. They reach into the sky, and blow in the wind, like pinwheels spinning on tall stems. Feel the warmth of the sun on your skin. It is just the right temperature for you. Notice the clouds passing overhead creating calming shadows as they go by. Picture the green grass swaying gently in the breeze.

As you take in a breath, let the air fill your lungs. Feel your stomach rise and fall with each full breath and exhalation. Each time you breathe out, feel yourself relaxing more and more. As you relax, your breathing slows. Rest quietly. Empty your mind of any worries.

With your mind's eye, find any spot inside your body that feels painful. Imagine that you can actually see the pain. The pain looks like a pile of stones stuck in your body.

Now focus your thoughts on one of the stones. You can move the stone away from your body with your breathing. Imagine that your breath has great strength. Feel your incredible strength each time you take in a breath.

Each time you breathe out, imagine that a jet of air lifts a stone, carries it out of your body, and sets it in the field of flowers. Look around the field of flowers and focus on one spot on the ground where you want to dump the stone. Each breath blows part of the pain away from you and sets it in a spot outside your body. Each stone is lifted away from the part of you that is feeling pain and the uncomfortable feeling gets smaller. Each breath brings more healing energy to you. Say to yourself: **"I am able to make myself feel comfortable."**

The size of the stone pile inside of you gets smaller, and the stone pile in the field gets bigger. Notice the size of each stone. Some stones are quite large and heavy. Some are light, more like pebbles. Each stone is part of the pain that you are strong enough to blow away from your body.

Breathe in strength. Breathe out pain. Each time you remove the pain, you notice that your body is filling the empty spot with your favorite color. With each stone you remove, you see more beautiful, vibrant color in its place.

As you see the stones leaving your body, you feel the pain leaving your body. The pain is now outside of you. Look at the pile of stones in the field. Colorful flowers are beginning to grow around them. A rainbow of flowers is surrounding the pile.

The flowers grow so tall that you cannot see the stones anymore. The stones are there but your eyes focus on the beautiful flowers. Take a deep breath and inhale the fresh fragrance of the flowers from your rock garden. Breathe deeply and say to yourself: **"I am able to make myself feel comfortable."**

(Coaching Note: *If your child is resting comfortably and you do not want to disturb him or her you can eliminate the next paragraphs.*)

When you are ready to return to the room, leave the rock pile in the field of flowers and take a deep breath. As you breathe out, open your eyes and come back to the room feeling comfortable and refreshed.

Whenever you would like to make your body feel comfortable, remember this story about making a stone pile in a field and seeing beautiful flowers grow around the stones.

You may wish to sniff some floral perfume or potpourri to help yourself remember the field of flowers. You may wish to draw a picture of the field with the colorful flowers filling it, and draw a picture of yourself with beautiful, healing colors filling you.

CANDLES

"I breathe in comfort and peace. I blow out difficulties and problems."

Coaching Notes: *In this story, a breathing exercise is explained by imagining blowing out a candle with brief bursts of air. This type of breathing can help you if you experience sharp pain.*

Take time to relax your muscles and take calm, peaceful breaths. Use the following paragraph or another of your choice.

Close your eyes gently, or focus on a picture or a spot near you.

Take a few moments to remember the last time you were relaxed and how good it felt. When you are comfortable, take a nice, deep breath. Notice how the air fills your body.

As you breathe out, let peaceful feelings move throughout your body. Let the rhythm of music calm you. Feel your muscles relax and your heartbeat and breathing slow.

> Say to yourself: "I am calm and relaxed."
> Take three slow breaths and each time you breathe out, relax all your muscles.

A special cake has been baked just for you. It is a beautiful, round, two-layer cake. Take a deep breath and sniff the fragrance of the frosting. The frosting is your favorite flavor. You cannot resist poking your finger into the frosting and taking a big lick of it. It's delicious!

The baker took special care to decorate the cake just for you. It is decorated with a scene of something you really enjoy. Make a picture in your mind of the decorations on top of this cake.

Although it is not your birthday, there are candles on top of this cake. When you have candles on your birthday cake, you take one big breath and try to blow out all your candles at once. In this story, the candles are different than birthday candles, and you will do a special kind of breathing so you only blow out one candle at a time. You will blow out short, strong puffs of air the way you blow out a match. Using your imagination to blow out each candle separately on this cake will help you blow away sad or scary thoughts, or uncomfortable feelings.

In your imagination, look at one of the candles on the top of your special cake. Focus on it alone. Take a breath, and as you do, watch the flame above the candle. Put your lips together and aim at the candle. With a strong puff, blow some air out of your lungs.

As you blow out the candle, let any sensations of discomfort, pain, fear, or sadness blow away with your breath. When you blow out those puffs of air, you blow out unwanted feelings. Say to yourself: **"I breathe in comfort and peace. I blow out difficulties and problems."**

The flame above the candle flickers and then goes out. Your

difficulties and problems are blown away and go out of you, too. Your mind feels rested and your body feels comfortable.

Take another breath and get your lips ready to blow out the next candle. Fill your lungs and let the air expand all the way to your stomach. Focus your mind on the candle flame. Watch the golden flame flicker back and forth above the candle.

Breathe out short bursts of air, blowing away all tingling or uncomfortable or painful sensations in your body. Watch the smoke drift away slowly into the air.

As you inhale, notice the faint smoky smell. Continue blowing out each candle one by one, taking time to think about what you are blowing away.

The cake has as many candles as you need for blowing out sharp pain or sad feelings. Imagine yourself blowing out a candle each time you want to blow away a feeling you would like to change.

With your inner voice, repeat three times: **"I breathe in comfort and peace. I blow out difficulties and problems."** As the smoke drifts away, you feel your problems drift away. Your body is relaxed from head to toe.

When you are ready to return to the room, take a deep breath. As you breathe out, open your eyes and drift back feeling relaxed. Whenever you want to blow away difficulties or problems remember the way you used your breathing in this story about the candles.

A FLAG

"I am happy, healthy, and strong."

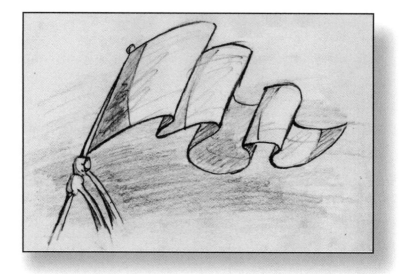

Coaching Notes: *In this story, you locate a spot inside your body that is painful or uncomfortable. You use your imagination to mark the spot with a flag. You focus your attention only on the movement of the flag and are distracted from the uncomfortable feeling below the flag.*

Flags can be found in many places. Boat owners often fly a flag at the back of their boat. Some people decorate their house with a flag, or banner, for the holidays. In times of war, a white flag indicates surrender. In car races, the flag-man waves different colored flags to give drivers information about the race. When explorers reach the top of a mountain, they stick a flag at the summit to represent their accomplishment. A flag can be used in many different ways.

Take time to relax your muscles and take calm, peaceful breaths.
Use the following paragraph or another of your choice.
Close your eyes gently, or focus on a picture or a spot near you.

Take a few moments to remember the last time you were relaxed and how good it felt. When you are comfortable, take a nice, deep breath. Notice how the air fills your body.

As you breathe out, let peaceful feelings move throughout your body. Let the rhythm of music calm you. Feel your muscles relax and your heartbeat and breathing slow.

Say to yourself: "I am calm and relaxed."

Take three slow breaths and each time you breathe out, relax all your muscles.

Most schools have a flag outside on display. On windy days, the large flag seems to dance in the sky. The red and white stripes and the white stars on the blue background seem to change shape as the flag flutters at the top of the flagpole.

Flag makers create flags to represent an idea. Colors are chosen carefully when a design is drawn. If you had a piece of white fabric in front of you what would you include in a design for your very own special flag?

Imagine making a design for your flag that represents you as a healthy, happy, and strong person. Think about the details you would put on your flag. What colors do you choose? What symbols tell about you? Take a few moments to design your flag in your imagination. When you can see your flag's design in your mind's eye, imagine attaching it to a pole that is just the right length for you to carry.

Imagine now that you are going on an unusual expedition. You will be taking a trip through the inside of your body. You are on an expedition to locate any spots inside of you that hurt. You have a backpack full of flags that you specially designed for your travels. In your hands, you have an assortment of poles to attach to your flags.

You are the person who makes the decisions on this trip, so you start traveling anywhere you wish inside your body. The trip is relaxing, but when you locate a painful spot, you have a plan of action. Take one of the poles you brought with you and imagine sticking the flagpole near the sensitive spot to mark it. Next, attach one of your specially designed flags to the pole. The design on the flag represents you as feeling healthy, happy, and strong. When you feel any pain, the eyes of your imagination go to your flag as it waves above the discomfort. Try that now. Let your eyes focus on the flag.

Take a deep breath and then gently blow out the air. Imagine your breath as a gentle wind catching your flag and causing it to wave. It makes you smile to see your flag dance in the wind. Take a few moments to breathe gently in and out, and to look at your flag waving above the discomfort. Say to yourself: **"I am healthy, happy, and strong."**

Watch your flag. Concentrate on the colors you used when you designed it. Notice how the flag changes shape as your breath moves it. The flag moves back and forth almost like the flame of a candle.

Continue to focus only on the flag. Continue to breathe in deeply and to move your flag as you breathe out. Repeat to yourself: **"I am healthy, happy, and strong."**

With your eyes on the flag, you are distracted from any uncomfortable sensations. When the pain is easier to handle, or gone completely, your flag rests quietly against its pole. Picture yourself moving away and continuing with your trip.

If you ever need to go back to that spot you will be able to find your flag that marks the spot. You can look above discomfort by focusing on your flag. It is your symbol of healing. Repeat to yourself again: **"I am healthy, happy, and strong."**

When you are ready to return to the room, take a deep breath. As you breathe out, open your eyes. You feel relaxed and refreshed. You know you will always be able to focus on healthy, happy, strong feelings in your body.

STORIES TO HELP WITH NAUSEA

> **Tips from Olivia, who has therapy to make her muscles stronger**
>
> If you have a stomachache, have soft Jell-O or something healthy and drink a lot of liquid. Hold a soft "lovey" to make your stomach feel soft and comfortable and then you can go to sleep.

UH-OH! It can happen on a roller coaster or a merry-go-round. It can happen in a car, boat, or plane. You might feel it when you are sick or when you eat way too much. It might happen when you take certain medicines. You know what I mean. It's that uneasy, icky feeling in your stomach, which may or may not lead to throwing up.

Your brain controls that queasy feeling in your stomach. Your brain is constantly getting messages from all parts of your body. Even when you are sleeping, your brain is taking messages and giving messages.

Smells, medicines, illnesses, and a number of other causes can give your brain the message to throw up. We sure don't like feeling sick to our stomach, so it's lucky for us that there are ways to control the messages that go to our brain. One way is to take a medicine that gives your brain the message to settle the uncomfortable feelings in your stomach.

Make Food Choices

Another thing to try is to carefully choose what you eat on days you think you might feel queasy. If you eat foods that are easy to digest your stomach does not have to work too hard. When you eat big meals you force your stomach to do a lot of work all at one time, so it is better to take it easy and eat smaller meals if you think you might feel sick to your stomach. Even though you may have an uneasy feeling in your stomach, it is still important for your body to get fluids, and the best way to do that is by drinking clear liquids.

Think of things that would taste good to you. Think of as many different foods, juices, and treats that you like. Make a list of them and ask them to be put on your family's shopping list. It will help you the next time you're trying to think of something good to eat or drink. Make your own menu!

Fighting Back

You have another helpful tool to use. It's one that you always carry with you. It's your brainpower! You can concentrate your thoughts on pleasant feelings instead of yucky-stomach feelings. You can distract your attention away from your queasy tummy to activities like games, puzzles, music, TV, or even gazing calmly out a window. You can fight nausea by sending messages to your brain that help you feel safe and relaxed. You can use positive statements about your stomach feeling settled down. Some examples of positive statements can be found in the next two stories.

Helpful Stories

Use the stories **"The Settlers"** and **"The Giraffe"** as tools to help yourself feel settled and in control of the feelings in your stomach.

Read the stories, **"Blast-Off!"** and **"A Flag"** for other positive statements about a calm stomach.

THE SETTLERS

"As I relax, my stomach settles down."

Coaching Notes: *Years ago, people rode in covered wagons and traveled over long, bumpy trails to settle in the west. In this story, you are taking a journey toward health with cues to settle an upset stomach.*

Take time to relax your muscles and take calm, peaceful breaths. Use the following paragraph or another of your choice.

Close your eyes gently, or focus on a picture or a spot near you.

Take a few moments to remember the last time you were relaxed and how good it felt. When you are comfortable, take a nice, deep breath. Notice how the air fills your body.

As you breathe out, let peaceful feelings move throughout your body. Let the rhythm of music calm you. Feel your muscles relax and your heartbeat and breathing slow.

Say to yourself: "I am calm and relaxed."
Take three slow breaths and each time you breathe out, relax all your muscles.

I magine being a traveler in a covered wagon. You are sitting on the seat at the front of the wagon, gazing out at the prairie ahead of you. All your belongings are packed in the wagon and you are eager to reach your new home.

On such a long trip, family members take turns driving the oxen team. It is your turn to drive. The reins of the oxen are in your hands and you set the pace of your trip.

Many wagon trains have traveled on this path and there are deep ruts in the trail. This part of the trail is very bumpy. The wagon moves you up and down over the uneven dirt path. The up and down motion of the wagon makes your stomach feel upset.

You notice another path alongside the one you are on. It is much smoother. Fewer wagons have traveled on it and there are no deep ruts. You are the driver and you decide to steer the oxen over to the flat road and travel on the steady, smooth path.

As soon as you are on the new trail, the bouncing and bumping stops and you are able to steady your body and smooth out the feeling in your stomach. The trail goes on as far as your eyes can see and you focus your eyes far ahead. Look straight ahead, far down the trail. This stills your eyes and stills the feeling in your stomach.

There is a gentle breeze that washes over your face and keeps you cool. Tilt your face upward to the blue sky and catch the fresh wind on your body. Each time you breathe, fill your lungs with a breath of clean, cool air. The cool air helps your stomach settle down. Filling your lungs steadies your body on the bumpy trail. Take a breath and say to yourself: **"As I relax, my stomach settles down."**

The wagon settles down and so does the feeling in your stomach. The wheels glide along the trail. You know this trail will take you to a place where you will feel comfortable and healthy. Repeat to yourself: **"As I relax, my stomach settles down."**

Now imagine relaxing your arms and legs because it takes so little effort to steer the wagon on this smooth path. Relax the muscles in your stomach. Let your stomach gently stretch with each breath.

The wind is cool on your forehead. As the wagon wheels move forward down the smooth trail, you sing a phrase over and over in your mind. You sing, **"As I relax, my stomach settles down."** Chant the words over and over, and as you sing, feel your stomach calm down.

Steady, slow breathing calms your stomach. Continue to breathe in the cool air and let the motion in your stomach roll out of you each time you breathe out. You are on the road to healing.

Keep your eyes focused far ahead on the long trail. Fill your eyes with the colors of the flowers along the trail. The purple coneflowers greet you. The tall, yellow sunflowers seem to smile at you as you roll by. The rustle of the wind through the tall grass chants with you, **"As I relax, my stomach settles down."**

Watch an eagle glide smoothly through the air above, as you glide smoothly over the trail. Take a breath with the movement of the eagle's wings, then glide along the trail as the eagle glides smoothly in the air. It is a peaceful sight and peaceful feeling.

You are getting closer to making camp and resting for the night. When you stop for the day, climb out of the wagon and notice that the calm, steady feeling stays with you. Imagine now, walking around your campsite and watching the setting sun fill the sky with red and orange colors. You sleep outside with the stars and moon giving you light. You rest comfortably and wake up feeling refreshed.

When you are ready to return to the room, take a deep breath. As you breathe out, open your eyes. You feel refreshed and relaxed.

165

If your stomach ever feels upset, remember the steady feeling on the road to healing.

Gently stretch your stomach muscles with slow, gentle breaths. Breathe in and out with a steady rhythm. Use a cool cloth on your forehead and think about how the coolness on your face calms your whole body. Choose a path that helps your stomach feel steady. Think of the steady, smooth flight of an eagle as it glides through the sky.

THE GIRAFFE

"My breathing settles my stomach."

Coaching Notes: *In this story, you will focus on a rhythmic breathing pattern to help your stomach feel more comfortable. Then you will imagine a giraffe eating special mint leaves that soothe its stomach.*

> **Take time to relax your muscles and take calm, peaceful breaths.**
> Use the following paragraph or another of your choice.
> Close your eyes gently, or focus on a picture or a spot near you.

167

Take a few moments to remember the last time you were relaxed and how good it felt. When you are comfortable, take a nice, deep breath. Notice how the air fills your body.

As you breathe out, let peaceful feelings move throughout your body. Let the rhythm of music calm you. Feel your muscles relax and your heartbeat and breathing slow.

Say to yourself: "I am calm and relaxed."

Take three slow breaths and each time you breathe out, relax all your muscles.

Take a full breath and notice the gentle stretch as your lungs fill with air. Count slowly as you breathe in through your nose. "In-two-three." Expand your lungs and stomach until you feel a slight, gentle fullness. Then breathe out through your lips. "Out-two-three." Keep using this rhythm as long as it helps you feel better.

You may wish to add a movement with your finger to keep you focused on the steady rhythm. Move your finger back and forth like the motion of a windshield wiper to the beat of your breathing.

Focus your thoughts on your breathing and the pattern of your counting. In-two-three. Out-two-three. Brush away other thoughts the way windshield wipers brush away raindrops. Say to yourself three times: **"My breathing settles my stomach."**

Now use your imagination to picture yourself at the zoo standing outside the giraffe's home. The tall-necked giraffe is chewing leaves from the branches of a tree. Watch as the giraffe calmly and slowly chews. The chewing matches the rhythm of your breathing. Chomp-two-three. Breathe-two-three.

The giraffe's stomach is upset and chewing leaves calms it. The chewed leaves glide slowly and gently down the giraffe's long throat. The leaves are special, minty leaves and when they reach the stomach, they help the giraffe feel better.

Continue the rhythmic pattern of your breathing. Imagine that you have something special to chew that helps your stomach feel better. Imagine the good feeling in your mouth as you chomp and chew-two-three. Breathe-two-three. The pattern of your breathing and chewing brings comfort to you.

Pretend that your throat is as long as the giraffe's. Imagine that your stomach is far away from your mouth, giving time for your special formula to soothe you as you chew it and it glides down your long throat.

Use this breathing for as long as you choose, to help yourself feel better.

When you are ready to return to the room, take a deep breath. As you breathe out, open your eyes. You feel refreshed and relaxed. Your stomach is calm and steady. When you want to calm your stomach, remember the rhythm of the breathing pattern in this story. Imagine your stomach being far from your mouth. You can try using a mint to suck on, or gum to chew, when you think about the giraffe.

THINKING ABOUT TAKING MEDICINE

> **Tips from Brianna, who was treated for cancer**
>
> Put chocolate syrup in the pink medicine (TMP sulfa), it makes it taste a little better.

Your body has a way to fight diseases and keep them away. It is called your immune system. Your immune system is like an army that defends you from disease. The soldiers in your army are your white blood cells. They are called lymphocytes. They do the job of checking out germs, viruses, bacteria, and abnormal cells that show up in your body.

If something unhealthy gets into your system the white blood cells go into action. They can gobble up bacteria, zap germ cells, or stop cancer cells from growing. They are a powerful part of your body. But even such a powerful system can become overwhelmed or tired. For instance, if too many germs or cancer cells are in your body at one time your immune system needs help. That's where medicine comes in handy. It brings more strength for your immune system so it can continue the fight.

Sometimes the cells of your immune system become confused and they attack healthy cells in your body by mistake. If they do this it can make you sick and cause a number of serious illnesses called auto-immune diseases. Medicines also come in handy for these illnesses.

Medicine Creates Change

Medicine can help a person become healthier and feel more comfortable. There are hundreds of different kinds of medicine and each one can help a person in some way. Doctors are trained to know which medical drugs to prescribe to help you.

If you are taking medicine, it helps to know in what way the medicine is working in your body. If you are not certain, be sure to ask so you can understand why it is important for you to take the medicine.

The other thing you should check is if your medication has side effects. What if a medicine you're taking makes you extra sleepy, or nauseated, or over-excited and it is hard for you to get to sleep? Wouldn't you want to know, so you wouldn't have to worry about why you feel the way you do? Again, be sure to ask.

Some people may experience side effects that affect their stomachs, which may change their appetite. Other side effects may change the way a person looks for awhile, including hair loss or a change in weight. Some medicines may cause changes in the number of blood cells that fight infection. Not everyone experiences side effects, but your nurses and doctors will explain the changes that may occur and will tell you how to take care of the changes in your body.

It helps to be able to talk about how you feel when you take medicine so your family and nurses can make you as comfortable as possible. Your parents, nurses, and doctors can reassure you that if you feel sick from your treatments, it does not mean the illness you are being treated for is getting worse. It helps to think of the side effects as signals that the medicine is in your body and is working on your cells. Life changes for a while. It is a time to be patient with your treatments and their side effects. Remember that side effects will gradually go away when all your treatments are finished.

Medicine Comes in Many Forms

There are so many different ways to get medicine into your body. There are sprays, inhalers, creams, pills, liquids — and that's just to name a few. Another way is through an injection, usually called a "shot." In the hospital, a common method is the use of a central line, also called an IV.

Sometimes it might sound like the person is saying the word "ivy," like the plant "poison ivy," but they are really saying IV, an abbreviation of the word *intravenous*. The IV medicine comes in a clear, plastic bag. The bag is hooked to a tall, metal pole that has wheels on the bottom so it can be moved around. A long, plastic tube reaches from the bag to the person. On the tip of the tube is a needle that is inserted into one of your veins.

A nurse programs a computer that lets the IV machine know how much medicine you need and how fast the medicine should drip through the tube that is attached to your body. After the needle poke, there is no discomfort from an IV. You can fall asleep with an IV, or take a walk outside your room, or do many other things that you enjoy.

Some people receive strong medicine through a small tube called a catheter that is placed under their skin. Then the IV can be connected directly into the catheter, which leads directly to a vein.

What Happens When Medicine Goes Inside Your Body?

When you take medicine, it travels in your blood vessels to places all through your body. Blood vessels are like tiny tubes. In less than one minute, blood can make a round trip throughout your body. This is called the circulation of the blood. Your blood goes round and round in your body. Your blood carries food and oxygen to your body's cells and takes waste products away from the cells. It also carries the medicine that you are taking.

Sometime after you have started treatments, your doctor will order more blood tests. For some people this might be every day, or every week, or every few months. When a blood test is taken, your doctor checks the number of white blood cells, red blood cells, and platelets in your blood. This is called your blood count. Your doctor gains information from your blood count about how things are going inside your body and how well the medicine is working.

Stick to Your Schedule

Most medicines have to be taken on a specific schedule — every few hours — once a day — or even once a month. Schedules vary, but it is important to stick to the schedule so the drug can do its best work for you.

Let's say you're playing a game with your friends and you are all taking turns. If someone just decides to quit, it often ruins the game. Don't let your medicine quit. Be sure you take it when the schedule says you need to, even if you feel like you don't want to.

The length of time you need to keep taking your medicine also varies. Sometimes you only have to take a certain prescription one time or perhaps just for a few days. Other prescriptions seem to go on for a really long time — even years! Each type has its own job to do, and you need to stick with it even if you are feeling better and it doesn't seem like you need medicine anymore. It might be a type of medicine that has the job of keeping disease away.

Medicines Do Important Work

Once you start a treatment plan, stick with it even if you feel like you want to quit. Think of a caterpillar inside a cocoon. We cannot see the changes going on inside of the cocoon but we know it takes time for the changes to happen. The caterpillar cannot come out early because it would not be finished growing into a butterfly.

When we take medicine, we cannot see the changes happening inside our bodies but that does not mean we can stop taking the medicine early. The treatment plan needs time to work. We need enough time for all the important changes to occur that are part of our healing.

When you take medicine do your very best to relax. Concentrate your thoughts on how it will help your body. I have to take several medicines every day. Each morning when I hold them in my hand I take a few moments to think about how thankful I am that these medicines have been discovered and are available to help me become healthier. I know that research will continue and that new and even better medicines will be invented soon.

Chemotherapy and Cancer

Some children who have cancer take strong medicines called chemotherapy. The goal of chemotherapy is to stop the growth of unhealthy cells inside a person. When the medicine reaches cancer cells, the growth of those cells is changed and the cells eventually die.

Researchers have discovered many medicines that can kill cancer cells. The drugs usually have long, strange sounding names. Your treatments will be designed especially for you and may include a combination of drugs. Your doctor decides which medicines will help you. Most people have treatments over a period of several months.

As the medicine damages the cancer cells, some of the healthy cells in a person's body may also become weakened. When normal cells change, it is called a side effect of chemotherapy. Side effects are not caused by the illness, but they may happen as a result of the treatment. A side effect usually depends on the type of medicine that is being used. Some side effects happen right away and others may occur days or weeks after chemotherapy has begun.

Relaxing Before and During Chemotherapy

Chemotherapy treatments are usually given at the hospital or clinic and they can last for several hours. Before you have chemotherapy, you can use relaxation and active imagination stories to help yourself get ready. Keep positive statements in your mind about staying comfortable and about healing. Concentrate on all the care that is being given to you to help your body heal quickly. Take relaxing breaths to help your body feel calm and ready for the medicine.

If listening to music helps you stay calm, bring a CD or tape player with you to your treatments. You might like to bring along a special toy or game. It's nice to have a joke or two to share with others. A smile helps people feel good.

Helpful Stories

The stories **"Rainbow"** and **"Snowflakes"** can help you think about medicine in a positive way.

The stories **"Putting Out Fires," "Soccer Victory,"** and **"Chalk Drawing"** help you use your imagination to think about medicine working to make you healthier. In some of the stories, you gently wash away disease, while in other stories you smash and destroy unhealthy cells. Choose a way that works for you when you visualize unhealthy cells going away. Use any ideas from your own imagination, too.

The stories **"Blast-Off!," "Ship Deck,"** and **"Aquarium"** offer ideas about getting ready for a chemotherapy appointment.

STORIES ABOUT TAKING MEDICINE

RAINBOWS

"The medicine I take brightens my body with healing."

Coaching Notes: *Doctors prescribe medicine to fight disease and to calm pain. In this story, imagine some of your favorite flavors that match the colors of the rainbow. Think about swallowing these delicious tastes to make a rainbow in your stomach. Keep your rainbow in your mind when you take your medicine.*

Take time to relax your muscles and take calm, peaceful breaths.
Use the following paragraph or another of your choice.

Close your eyes gently, or focus on a picture or a spot near you.

Take a few moments to remember the last time you were relaxed and how good it felt. When you are comfortable, take a nice, deep breath. Notice how the air fills your body.

As you breathe out, let peaceful feelings move throughout your body. Let the rhythm of music calm you. Feel your muscles relax and your heartbeat and breathing slow. Say to yourself: "I am calm and relaxed."

Take three slow breaths and each time you breathe out, relax all your muscles.

Before you take medicine, imagine a rainbow of colors going down your throat and filling your stomach, and then filling your whole body with bright colors. Imagine flavors that match the colors of the rainbow. Picture bright colors of red, orange, yellow, green, blue, and purple. Think of something wonderful that you love to eat or drink that matches each of these colors.

What do you love to taste that is the color red? Make a picture of it in your imagination. Now imagine holding it in your hand, looking at it, and carefully noticing every detail. Bring it up to your nose and sniff it. Imagine the fragrance of your red treat. Thinking of your delicious red treat makes your mouth water. Your tongue is happy to welcome it into your body. Take a bite and let the flavor slide down your throat. The red color fills your body.

Do the same thing with each color of the rainbow. Repeat the process of seeing it, sniffing it, feeling it in your mouth and tasting the favorite flavor, then letting it slide down your throat until it fills your body.

What do you love to taste that is the color orange? Make a picture of it in your imagination. Hold it in your hand and look at it carefully noticing every detail. Bring it up to your nose and sniff it. Imagine the fragrance of your orange treat. Thinking of your delicious orange treat makes your mouth water. Your tongue is happy to welcome it into your body. Take a bite and let the flavor slide down your throat. The orange color joins the color red inside your body.

What do you love to taste that is the color yellow? Make a picture of it in your imagination. Hold it in your hand and look at it carefully noticing every detail. Bring it up to your nose and sniff it. Imagine the fragrance of your yellow treat. Thinking of your delicious yellow treat makes your mouth water. Your tongue is happy to welcome it into your body. Take a bite and let the flavor slide down your throat. It joins the other colors.

What do you love to taste that is the color green? Make a picture of it in your imagination. Hold it in your hand and look at it carefully noticing every detail. Bring it up to your nose and sniff it. Imagine the fragrance of your green treat. Thinking of your delicious green treat makes your mouth water. Your tongue is happy to welcome it into your body. Take a bite and let the flavor slide down your throat.

What do you love to taste that is the color blue? Make a picture of it in your imagination. Hold it in your hand and look at it carefully noticing every detail. Bring it up to your nose and sniff it. Imagine the fragrance of your blue treat. Thinking of your delicious blue treat makes your mouth water. Your tongue is happy to welcome it into your body. Take a bite and let the flavor slide down your throat.

What do you love to taste that is the color purple? Make a picture of it in your imagination. Hold it in your hand and look at it carefully noticing every detail. Bring it up to your nose and sniff it. Imagine the fragrance of your purple treat. Thinking of your delicious purple treat makes your mouth water. Your tongue is happy to welcome it into your body. Take a bite and let the flavor slide down your throat.

Now that you have imagined swallowing all the delicious colors, picture them making a rainbow inside your body. The good tastes of the rainbow fill your taste buds until there is no room left for unpleasant tastes. Now you are ready to swallow your medicine. Imagine swallowing the pill or liquid. It glides down your throat to join your rainbow. You are able to take medicine without difficulties. Say to yourself: **"The medicine I take brightens my body with healing."**

The healing medicine joins with the rainbow colors flowing through your body to fight disease or to make your body feel more comfortable. The rainbow flavors make you feel good. Your medicine makes you feel good too, but in a different way: a healing way. A rainbow brightens up the sky. Your medicine brightens up your body. Repeat to yourself three times, **"The medicine I take brightens my body with healing."**

When you are ready to return to the room, take a deep breath. As you breathe out, open your eyes and feel refreshed and relaxed. Taking medicine is one of the ways you can help your body heal.

SNOWFLAKES

"Healing is happening inside my body."

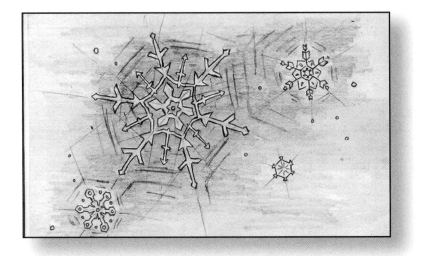

Coaching Notes: *This story gives you a way to think about the healing that is occurring inside your body. You can use your imagination to compare the snowflakes to the way your immune system gets help from the medicine you take to become healthier.*

Take time to relax your muscles and take calm, peaceful breaths. Use the following paragraph or another of your choice.

Close your eyes gently, or focus on a picture or a spot near you.

Take a few moments to remember the last time you were relaxed and how good it felt. When you are comfortable, take a nice, deep breath. Notice how the air fills your body.

As you breathe out, let peaceful feelings move throughout your body. Let the rhythm of music calm you. Feel your muscles relax and your heartbeat and breathing slow.

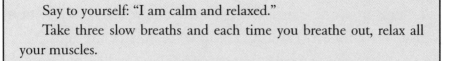

181

> Say to yourself: "I am calm and relaxed."
> Take three slow breaths and each time you breathe out, relax all your muscles.

Gently, gently snowflakes fall. They begin far above your head and you watch them float toward your body. As they slowly fall from above, your breathing slows and matches the gentle descent of the snowflakes. Gentle breathing in and out.

At each spot where a snowflake touches you, your muscles relax. Catch a snowflake on your nose. Feel the cool relaxation drift to the muscles in your face. Snowflakes land on your arms and hands. Release all tension from your upper body. Your arms, hands and fingers feel loose. The gentle touch of the snowflakes landing on your legs signals your muscles to let go of all tightness. The snowflakes cover you like a lacey quilt.

Imagine watching the white snowflakes float from above and touch your body. Gentle breathing, floating, relaxing. The snowflakes increase and your peaceful feelings increase. Now you are ready to use the snowflakes to imagine a way to help heal your body. Let the snowfall get heavier on your body and imagine letting the snowflakes sink through your skin, into your body.

Find any places inside of you that need to be healthier. Breathe in, and when you softly blow out the air, imagine sending the snowflakes to the spots in your body that need to be healthier. The snowfall increases in those spots. Watch the snowdrifts become deeper with each breath. The snow is piling up in places inside your body that need to be healed.

Enough flakes fall on you so that your white blood cells, the healing immune cells in your body, gather together like children who love to play in the snow. Watch the cells in your body smiling with happiness as they playfully make snow angels, snow forts, and snow-balls. Your immune cells are active throughout your body. Repeat to yourself three times: **"Healing is happening inside my body."**

The snow piles are cold. They trap and freeze the unhealthy cells. The piles block the roadways to the unhealthy spots. The roadways in your body are the blood vessels. Imagine snow clogging the pathways so the unhealthy cells can't escape. They are also cut off from their food sources. They become weak.

Your active immune system cells continue to surround the piles of freezing snow and when that happens, the unhealthy cells are destroyed. Your white blood cells scoop up the damaged cells in the snow and make snowballs and toss them far outside your body. The tossing goes on and on as the unhealthy cells are removed from your body.

You call in the snow blowers to get rid of snowdrifts that are filled with all the trapped unhealthy cells. Watch as the snow blowers dig through the drifts, and with great force, imagine them blowing the snow and sick cells out of you. The snow blowers clear the unhealthy spots in your body and clear the blood vessel roadways. Your body weathers the storm. You are refreshed. Your immune system is ready for more action.

When you are ready to return to the room, take a deep breath. As you breathe out, open your eyes and feel refreshed and relaxed. Remember this story when you want to think about the healing that is taking place inside your body.

PUTTING OUT FIRES

"The medicine I take helps my body heal."

Coaching Notes: *In this story, imagine being a firefighter who puts out a fire by spraying water onto it. The idea is compared to the effects of medicine helping to eliminate disease. You will imagine that the medicine you take is putting out the "fires" (unhealthy cells) in your body.*

Take time to relax your muscles and take calm, peaceful breaths. Use the following paragraph or another of your choice.

Close your eyes gently, or focus on a picture or a spot near you.

Take a few moments to remember the last time you were relaxed and how good it felt. When you are comfortable, take a nice, deep breath. Notice how the air fills your body.

As you breathe out, let peaceful feelings move throughout your body. Let the rhythm of music calm you. Feel your muscles relax and your heartbeat and breathing slow.

> Say to yourself: "I am calm and relaxed."
> Take three slow breaths and each time you breathe out, relax all your muscles.

Sirens are blaring. Bright lights are flashing. A red fire truck speeds by. Somewhere a family is in trouble and firefighters are on their way to help. The driver knows exactly where to go and the fire engine arrives within a few minutes.

When the firefighters arrive, they see a house burning. Flames shoot out from windows in the house. Each firefighter has a different job to do. One firefighter connects the hoses to the hydrant and a strong stream of water rushes through it. Other firefighters point the hoses toward the fiery spots.

The cold, rushing water is so strong and powerful that each burning spot is quickly put out. The emergency is over. The house will need some repair work but the thankful family will be able to move back into their home. They are safe.

Now use your imagination to think about your body being like the house. Your body needs some help right now. You are fighting an illness and your family has called for help. Your help does not come on a bright red fire engine. It comes in a hospital or medical office. The people at the hospital and doctor's office know what your body needs. When you see your nurse or doctor, you know you are safe.

Imagine that you are getting ready to take medicine or have a chemotherapy treatment. Begin by focusing on your breathing. Take a deep breath and feel your body fill with the energy you need for the job you are about to do. Blow the air out of your lungs with a soft sound to release any nervousness. Take one more deep breath and gently release the air by blowing out with a soft sound. When you feel refreshed and relaxed, your body is ready to go to work.

With your eyes closed, imagine the unhealthy cells in your body as very small fires. The fires need to be put out so they do not get bigger and destroy healthy cells near them. Think about the medicine that you swallow, or that comes to you through an injection or an IV, as water that comes in a hose to put out fires. Make a picture in your mind of the medicine squirting out, full force, at the little fires. See the medicine working.

The medicine is streaming through your veins and doing the job you want it to do. It travels through every part of your body, wherever it needs to be. You are glad you are having a treatment today.

You are calm because you want to give the medicine time to go where it needs to go. Take gentle breaths in, and breathe out gently, relaxing your muscles as you breathe calmly and peacefully.

In your imagination, take a moment to watch the damaged cells die. The "water" from your hose has smothered the fires. Where there used to be hot spots, now there are only cool, healthy cells. The hot spots have been reduced to smoke and ashes and your healthy body cleans them out and gets rid of them. Breathe out the smoke and breathe in clear, fresh air. Say to yourself three times: **"The medicine I take helps my body heal."**

When you are ready to return to the room, take a breath of fresh air. As you breathe out, open your eyes. Your body feels relaxed. Whenever you take medicine, think back to this story. Remember that healing occurs inside of you and your body knows what to do. You can extinguish unhealthy cells. Being a firefighter is a big job. You are thankful for the people around you who are helping you today. You have a big team of people working to help you. When today's job is done, you feel proud of yourself.

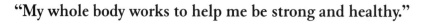

SOCCER VICTORY

"My whole body works to help me be strong and healthy."

Coaching Notes: *In this story, you will think about the healthy cells in your body working together as teammates to be winners against disease. Drops of medicine are compared to soccer balls. You will make a picture in your mind of kicking the medicine into the goal to defeat disease. You will see yourself surrounded by a strong team whenever you take medicine or chemotherapy. When your team scores, you will feel excited.*

Before you take medicine or begin a chemotherapy treatment, take some time to think about being a soccer player. A soccer player prepares for a big game. You can prepare for your appointment by thinking about the way your body works when you take medicine. You may want to wear your soccer jersey or a favorite shirt to a chemotherapy appointment to help yourself concentrate on this story.

Take time to relax your muscles and take calm, peaceful breaths.
Use the following paragraph or another of your choice.
Close your eyes gently, or focus on a picture or a spot near you.

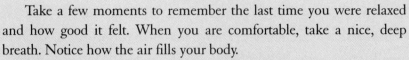

> Take a few moments to remember the last time you were relaxed and how good it felt. When you are comfortable, take a nice, deep breath. Notice how the air fills your body.
>
> As you breathe out, let peaceful feelings move throughout your body. Let the rhythm of music calm you. Feel your muscles relax and your heartbeat and breathing slow.
>
> Say to yourself: "I am calm and relaxed."
>
> Take three slow breaths and each time you breathe out, relax all your muscles.

With your eyes closed, make a picture in your mind of a large, grassy soccer field. Walk confidently onto the grass and get ready for the game to begin. Breathe deeply and smell the fresh grass. The crisp air fills your lungs and gives you energy. Breathe out any nervousness before the game. Tighten, then relax your hands and feet. Give them a little shake to loosen them even more.

Expand your lungs and imagine breathing in the blue color of the sky. The sky is so blue that being outside makes you smile. Look around the field and notice the colors around you; the green grass, bright uniforms, white clouds. Watching the gentle clouds moving across the sky helps your breathing stay slow and relaxed.

You are ready. The game is about to begin. Watch the other players walk onto the field, and notice that today you have very special teammates. In today's game, your teammates are the millions of healthy cells that travel throughout your body. The soccer field is filled with your healthy cells that are ready to help you win your game.

Your team members are alert and ready for victory. They are lined up throughout the field ready for the game to begin. What a great game this will be!

As your treatment begins, the ref blows the whistle to start the game. This is no ordinary game of soccer! Imagine that each drop of your medicine is a soccer ball that moves through your body. Your cells move the balls forward with incredible skill. They can spin and dodge and head the balls. They can dribble with amazing speed and control. They are all aiming for a special goal — your goal of being healthy.

Your team speeds through your body. Feel the warmth and energy of millions of teammates, each kicking balls of medicine toward the goal. You are glad it is a game day and you are confident as the medicine enters your body. Say to yourself three times, **"My whole body works to help me be strong and healthy."**

Imagine any unhealthy cells all clustered together inside the goal net. The unhealthy cells are confused. They do not know how to play the game. They do not spread out as your healthy cells do. They clump together. They make an easy target. Soccer players focus on the net as they pass the ball back and forth looking for the opportunity to score.

Your coach shouts encouragement and cheers for your team. "Keep running. You can do it. GO. GO. GO." You have endless energy. The momentum is in your favor. A ball soars off a foot, passes the goalie, and zooms into the net. Player after player aims a strong kick to the net. Player after player scores. The crowd cheers like crazy.

Your team demolishes the unhealthy cells. The balls of medicine travel throughout your body guided by the strong kicks of your team, and they pound all unhealthy cells. The unhealthy cells are flattened. They are destroyed. What a game! It is a great feeling to take medicine that helps your body win against disease.

When you are ready to return to the room, take a deep breath. As you breathe out, open your eyes. You feel refreshed and relaxed. If you feel thirsty and hungry and tired, think about ways to refresh yourself. You are taking care of yourself on and off the field.

189

Stay relaxed and enjoy your victory!

Look ahead to your next treatment and know that once again you will win. Think about the excitement that you feel as you play this game. It is a great feeling to play a game and walk off the field with a victory. As you leave after such a big day, you feel the satisfaction that comes from doing a good job.

CHALK DRAWING

"Each day of treatment helps me become healthy."

Coaching Notes: *In this story, you will make a picture in your mind of the medicine you take washing away germs or unhealthy cells, the way rain washes away a chalk drawing on the sidewalk.*

Take time to relax your muscles and take calm, peaceful breaths.
Use the following paragraph or another of your choice.
Close your eyes gently, or focus on a picture or a spot near you.

Take a few moments to remember the last time you were relaxed and how good it felt. When you are comfortable, take a nice, deep breath. Notice how the air fills your body.

As you breathe out, let peaceful feelings move throughout your body. Let the rhythm of music calm you. Feel your muscles relax and your heartbeat and breathing slow.

Say to yourself: "I am calm and relaxed."

Take three slow breaths and each time you breathe out, relax all your muscles.

Imagine that it is a warm, summer day with gray clouds floating in the sky. Imagine yourself sitting outside on the sidewalk coloring a beautiful chalk drawing. You have a large collection of chalk in front of you. Some of the pieces are small because they are your favorite colors and you use them a lot, but you have every color that you need to create a picture.

Today you are making a picture of yourself and you are using all the colors you love. You start by making an outline of your body. Draw your head and neck, next your shoulders, arms and body, then your legs and feet. As you draw each line, you notice that the muscles in each part of your body relax. Take your time drawing your picture. As you draw, your breathing slows and you feel peaceful. Enjoy this feeling.

Your outline is done. Now, imagine coloring the inside of your body. Use chalk colors that make you think of being happy and healthy. Take your time. Breathe in and out, gently and calmly. You create an excellent picture. Step back, and admire your drawing.

Now a rain cloud gathers overhead. Raindrops begin to sprinkle the sidewalk. The gentle drops fall on your chalk drawing and as they do, the chalk colors run together. The rain makes the colors inside your artwork swirl together and blurs them. The soft rain continues falling from the cloud and eventually the picture is gone.

Now imagine that it is time for you to take medicine or have a chemotherapy treatment. Think of the medicine going into your body and finding the part of your body that needs to be healthier. The unhealthy cells look like gray dots of chalk inside your drawing. See the healing energy finding the gray dots.

As the medicine you are taking gently drips into your body, imagine it is like raindrops falling from the clouds above you. Imagine that the medicine dripping into your body rinses away the unhealthy cells, the way rain rinses away your drawing. You feel the healing changes happening in your body.

Each time you take medicine or have a treatment, think of the rain. Think of cancer cells or germs being rained on and then disappearing. Think of the sounds that raindrops make when they hit your window, the roof, the street, and your umbrella. Use the sounds to imagine the raindrops falling inside your body, either gently or as a torrential storm, to wash away disease.

Imagine the sound pouring into your body. It falls on your head, through your shoulders, arms and chest, down through your hips and thighs. Imagine the rain running through you in rivulets out through your feet, taking away illness, leaving you cleansed from the rain, from each drip and drop that gathers force with the others to create a powerful stream of healing.

After the rain storm ends, look at your drawing again. With your most brilliant colors, fill in the faded spots. The bright colors show that you are healthy. Say to yourself three times: **"Each day of treatment helps me become healthy."**

When you are ready to return to the room, take a deep breath. As you breathe out, open your eyes. You feel refreshed and relaxed. Water dissolves things, water cleans things, and water refreshes things. Think about rain that falls gently, as well as rain that pours down in a storm when you think about medicine in your body.

THINKING ABOUT SURGERY

Sometimes a child needs to have surgery. Having surgery is also called "having an operation." Surgery can help you become healthier when the surgeon takes a tumor out of your body or when a surgeon fixes something inside your body. People have surgery for other reasons too. Another reason to have surgery is to help a doctor learn if there have been changes to cells inside your body. This is called a biopsy. During this type of surgery, some cells are removed and then they are examined under a microscope. The doctor who looks at the cells is called a pathologist.

You can have surgery as an outpatient, which means you will go home shortly after surgery, or you could have surgery as an inpatient, which means you will stay overnight at the hospital. If you need to have surgery, you will usually have a few days to get ready for it. You might have a chance to visit the hospital and meet some of the people who will work with you in the operating room.

New Sights, Sounds, and Smells

If you have never seen an operating room, you are in for some surprises. The operating room, sometimes called the O.R. for short, will probably seem large to you. It will have equipment and machines that will be used to help you. Be prepared for new smells and sounds. You will notice big lights on the ceiling. The bright lights allow the surgeons to see everything clearly so there are no shadows while they work.

Nurses and doctors will be with you in the operating room quietly doing their jobs. Everyone in the room is there to help you in some way. You can help too, by focusing on taking relaxing breaths and relaxing your muscles. If surgery is a new experience for you, even if you have been told all about it beforehand, it may still seem strange to you. So if you have questions, it is fine to ask someone.

Preparing for Surgery

Every person who comes into the operating room is careful to avoid bringing in any germs. Your doctors and nurses wash their hands with special soap. They cover their hair with special caps and they wear special clothing. In operating rooms, people wear surgical masks so that they do not breathe any germs on you.

Your nurse will help you get ready for the operating room by cleaning the part of your body where surgery will be performed with a strong, smelly soap and an antibacterial liquid. Your hair may be covered with a surgical cap and you will be dressed in hospital clothes that have been carefully washed. Everything in the O.R. is really clean to help prevent infections of any kind.

Relaxing Before Surgery

Before you have surgery, you can use relaxation and active imagination stories to help yourself get ready for the operating room. Keep positive thoughts in your mind about staying comfortable and about healing. Concentrate on all the care you are receiving that will help your body heal quickly.

Listening to music is another way that you can help yourself stay calm. If you want to take a tape player or CD player into the operating room, check ahead of time to see if special headphones are needed. Listen to a favorite song. You can hum the music inside your head.

You can ask a nurse or your parent to talk to you as you get ready for surgery and, if you wish, they will hold your hand. Once all the preparations are completed, the time will seem to go very quickly.

Staying Comfortable During Surgery

Amid all these new experiences, there is something that will make you very happy — you will be comfortable during surgery. Doctors, called anesthesiologists, have medicine that you will take so you are comfortable and sleepy.

The anesthesiologist makes sure that you have just the right amount of medicine so you stay asleep during the whole surgery. The medicine, called an anesthetic, is given to you through an IV line in your hand or arm, or it might be given to you through a tube and small mask near your nose and mouth. You will breathe regularly with all the air you need, but, you will also breathe in medicine that will make you sleep through surgery.

After you fall asleep, a thin, flexible tube may be placed in your throat to help you breathe. The tube will be taken out before you wake up, but after surgery you may notice a sore feeling in your throat from the tube.

During surgery, everything in your body is still working just the way it does when you are awake. Your heart beats, your lungs breathe, your brain sends and receives messages. The difference is that you don't notice any of those things because you are sleeping soundly, thanks to the medication.

After Surgery

After surgery, you will be taken to a different room called a recovery room. You are not alone when you wake up. Nurses are nearby to help you. A nurse will be talking to you and checking your body.

You may have a bandage where you had surgery. The bandage is often called a dressing. Your nurse will check your dressing and your stitches, if you needed any. Another word for stitches is sutures. Sometimes the surgeon uses little clips called surgical staples instead of sutures to close an incision. You will be given medicine to help you feel comfortable as your body adjusts to the surgery.

When you wake up, you will be able to see your family again. Your nurse will give your parents information about how to take care of you as your body heals. The nurse will be able to tell when you are ready to leave the recovery room. If you will be staying in the hospital, you will ride back to your room on a bed with wheels. If you are going home, you will ride in a wheelchair to your car, which helps you save your energy for the trip ahead.

Helpful Stories

The stories **"Sand Sieve"** and **"A Tree"** are helpful to read when thinking about changes that may occur as a result of having surgery.

Read **"A Turtle"** and **"Dolphins"** to help you prepare for anesthesia before surgery or procedures requiring sedation.

"Ship Deck" and **"Blast Off!"** help you relax and have calm feelings before surgery.

"Peaceful Swamp" helps you rest quietly on a treatment table.

Read the **"Progressive Muscle Relaxation"** scripts to help yourself become relaxed as you prepare for surgery.

198

STORIES ABOUT SURGERY

SAND SIEVE

"I am filled with healthy cells."

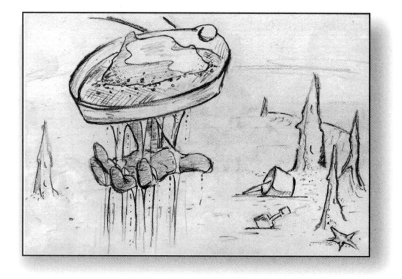

Coaching Notes: *You can make pictures in your mind of your body getting healthy. Imagine that you're going to the beach! Pack the cooler. Grab your towel, your beach toys, and the sunscreen. In this story, a sand sieve is used as an image of the body ridding itself of unhealthy cells. The healing cells in the body are separated from the unhealthy cells in an effort to rid illness from the body.*

Take time to relax your muscles and take calm, peaceful breaths.
Use the following paragraph or another of your choice.

Close your eyes gently, or focus on a picture or a spot near you.

Take a few moments to remember the last time you were relaxed and how good it felt. When you are comfortable, take a nice, deep breath. Notice how the air fills your body.

199

> As you breathe out, let peaceful feelings move throughout your body. Let the rhythm of music calm you. Feel your muscles relax and your heartbeat and breathing slow. Say to yourself: "I am calm and relaxed."
>
> Take three slow breaths and each time you breathe out, relax all your muscles.

It is a warm, sunny day and you are lying on your towel at the beach. Imagine the sounds of the waves as they lap onto the shore. Watch the shorebirds run beside you on their skinny legs. Smile at them as they scoot back and forth along the waves. Feel the sun soak into your skin as you stretch out and relax.

You are at a special beach with sand that is just perfect for building anything you like. You brought along the best bag of sand toys and you know you will create something wonderful with them. In the bag, you have a shovel, a pail, and a sieve. The sieve is like a shallow pan with a screen on the bottom. When you put sand on top of it, you can shake the sieve and the sand falls through the small holes.

Imagine beginning to play in the sand. The first thing you decide to make is a sandcastle. Not just any old castle, but one with fancy towers and a deep moat all around it. Scoop up the cool, damp sand and pat it into the shape of a fortress. Next, use the shovel to dig a moat all around your castle.

Now imagine scooping up some sand and putting it in your sieve. Gently shake your sieve and watch the fine grains of sand slip through the small holes. The strainer catches any pebbles, weeds, and sticks that are too big to slip through the small mesh holes. You don't want the junk that gets caught on the top of the screen, so you toss it far away from where you are sitting.

You love to watch the sand slip through the sieve, so you repeat the sifting process over and over. Soon you have a pile of soft, clean sand in front of you. Slip your fingers into the pile of sand and feel the softness run through your fingers. Now you have smooth, clean sand to spread all around your castle.

The small grains of sand on the beach help you think about the small cells that are inside your body. There are trillions of cells inside each of us, just like there are trillions of bits of sand on the beach. Think about your body, and say to yourself: **"I am filled with healthy cells."**

You have strong, healthy cells throughout every part of your body. Sometimes, there are cells inside of you that do not belong there. Your body works to get rid of them. Your immune system does this work every day to help you be healthy. Your immune system is made up of blood cells that know what cells belong inside of you and what cells do not belong. Your body knows how to grow and be strong. Take a moment to breathe gently, and concentrate on the work your body is doing to be healthy.

Continue to rest quietly in a comfortable position and think about your immune system cells inside your body getting rid of unhealthy cells. Repeat to yourself: **"I am filled with healthy cells."** See the bright sun shining on your body. Every part of you is light. From your head to your toes the sunshine surrounds every healthy cell in your body.

Imagine now, looking inside your body and noticing any unhealthy cells or germs. Pretend to scoop up some of the cells the way you would scoop up sand from the beach. Choose to begin at any part of your body. Imagine pouring the cells onto a sieve. In your imagination, gently shake the sieve back and forth. Imagine your cells beginning to bounce on top of the screen.

See your healthy cells fall freely through the mesh. The unhealthy cells, the ones you do not want, get caught on top of the mesh screen. Toss them far away from your body. Watch as your healthy cells spread out in your body. The healthy cells are healing you.

Repeat the sifting and tossing. Go to any part of your body that needs to have sick cells sifted out and tossed away. Say to yourself: **"I am filled with healthy cells."** Relax and appreciate the feeling of having healthy, healing cells throughout your body.

When you are ready to return to the room, take a deep breath. As you breathe out, open your eyes. You feel refreshed and relaxed. Your healthy cells are with you every day, ready to help you heal. Think about the warm sunny day at the beach and the feeling you have when your body is healing.

A TREE

"My body changes, and I am still me."

Coaching Notes: *In this story, you will use an image of a tree to give you a picture of strength that you can use whenever you wish to be strong. Sometimes a serious illness or a medication can have side effects that cause our bodies to change. This story helps remind us that even with changes in our appearance, we are still the people we were before.*

> **Take time to relax your muscles and take calm, peaceful breaths.** Use the following paragraph or another of your choice.
>
> Close your eyes gently, or focus on a picture or a spot near you.
>
> Take a few moments to remember the last time you were relaxed and how good it felt. When you are comfortable, take a nice, deep breath. Notice how the air fills your body.

203

As you breathe out, let peaceful feelings move throughout your body. Let the rhythm of music calm you. Feel your muscles relax and your heartbeat and breathing slow. Say to yourself: "I am calm and relaxed."

Take three slow breaths and each time you breathe out, relax all your muscles.

You are taking a walk in your favorite park. There are many trees in the park, but one of them is more special to you than the others. It stands strong and tall throughout all the seasons of the year. When you stand next to it, you feel strong and tall, too. Walk over to your tree and greet it. Put your hands on its trunk. How does it feel? Rest your cheek on its bark and notice the way it feels and smells. Lean back and look straight up into the tree. What do you see? Make a picture in your mind of your tree.

Look at the branches. Are there leaves on the branches? Are there any nests in the tree? When the breeze blows through your tree do you hear any sound? Do leaves whisper to you? Do branches creak as they bend in the wind? What season of the year is it? You can tell what season it is by describing the branches.

Next, imagine standing close to your tree and looking at your feet. Can you see the beginning of the tree's roots as they stretch into the ground? Do you see the ground swell where the roots grow under the tree? Imagine your feet becoming part of the roots that sink into the earth. The roots get the food that is needed to make the tree grow. Stand tall and strongly rooted next to your tree.

Now use your imagination to make a picture in your mind of your body growing as if it were a tree with roots, a trunk, and branches. You have roots at your feet, your body is like the tree trunk, and your head and arms are like branches covered with leaves. You are growing in a

place where you feel safe and protected. You are one of the trees in a quiet, sunny forest.

Your feet are rooted in the ground and you pull energy and nourishment up from the earth into your trunk. Your roots go deep into the earth and you feel energy flowing upward through your legs, to your stomach and chest, then through your arms and head.

Your arms and head reach up to the sun. Your leaves bring in the light. The light changes into energy for you through your leaves. Your leaves are a beautiful color from the energy of the light. They whisper and sway in the breeze, as do the leaves of the trees around you. Listen carefully for the messages from the other trees. As a breeze blows through the leaves on your branches, you give a message to the trees around you. Tell them something important about yourself.

A tree next to you has a broken limb. One of its branches was injured. Something happened to the branch and now it is shorter than the rest. The shape of the tree has changed. It is hard for anyone to notice the change, because other branches on the tree grew stronger and longer around it. Change is a natural part of life.

The tree with the broken limb is as beautiful as any other tree in the forest. Its roots reach as deeply into the earth. Its leaves reach upward and gather sunlight as well as any of the other trees. You know that a tree can grow and be strong, even when a branch is injured.

Your body can grow and be strong even if there is a part of it that needs to be changed during surgery to make the rest of your body healthier. Say to yourself three times: **"My body changes, and I am still me."**

When you are ready to return to your room, take a deep breath. As you breathe out, open your eyes. You feel refreshed and calm. If you are worried about changes in your body, imagine finding a special tree to visit, to think about, or to draw. Spend time with your tree, rest beneath it, and tell it things that are important to you. You know that trees change with the seasons and that you change, too.

THINKING ABOUT RADIATION THERAPY

Radiation therapy helps a person become healthier. It works by using invisible beams of high-energy x-rays to target unhealthy cells and prevent them from growing. All cells grow by splitting and becoming two cells, but cancer cells do not know when to stop splitting. They keep making more cells.

Radiation is a way of saying to the cells, **"STOP! NO MORE DIVIDING."** Radiation treatment is given in a small dose every day, usually for several weeks. This schedule allows the radiation to give the **STOP** message every day until all the cancer cells get the message. When the cells stop dividing, they die and the tumor shrinks.

When you have a treatment, about the only thing you will notice is a buzzing or humming sound coming from the machine. Otherwise there is nothing to feel, or smell, or taste, or see. Yet, radiation is very strong, so doctors plan carefully and use the right amount of radiation to make people healthier.

Sometimes the word *radiation* is used in cartoons, but that is not like the radiation in the hospital. The cartoon radiation is make-believe and in some cartoons it creates mutants or scary creatures. This does not happen in real life.

Preparing for Treatments

Your doctor makes many plans before your radiation treatments can begin. A special mold is created that fits your body and helps you stay in the same position for every treatment. A mold starts like a big beanbag. When it is shaped just right for your size, it is made stiff so it always keeps its shape for you. Your position is important because the part of your body to be treated is carefully measured.

The technician might paint a few dots or lines on your skin. Eventually the ink will wash off, but during radiation the spots will be part of a map to show the precise location where the radiation should be beamed. Some people actually get tiny, little dots tattooed onto their skin as part of their map.

Relaxing Before Radiation

Before you have a radiation treatment, you can use relaxation and active imagination stories to help yourself get ready. Keep positive statements in your mind about staying comfortable and about healing. Concentrate on all the care that is being given to you to help your body heal quickly. Taking relaxing breaths helps you feel calm and ready for the treatment room. Once the treatment starts, time will seem to go very quickly.

Use your imagination to think of ways to help yourself feel calm. Think about taking something into the treatment room that comforts you. You might like to wear a friendship bracelet or a pair of special socks, for example. Think of something that has special meaning to you. When you put it on you can begin to think of feeling calm and relaxed. Sometimes it is possible to play special music during your treatments. Music helps people feel comfortable.

A Brief Burst of Energy

The technicians place you on the treatment table and line up the spots with the aid of lasers and a computer. When the technicians have made all the correct adjustments, they will walk out of the room and stand near the door. At this time you will be alone in the room, but if you have any questions you may speak into a microphone and they will hear you outside the room.

You will only be on the treatment table for a few minutes, but during that time, a brief burst of energy will be aimed at the area of your body being treated. You will not feel a thing. The radiation beam comes out of a large machine that moves above and around the table. The machine will be moved close to your body but it will never touch you.

The machine is called a linear accelerator, or linac for short. It may seem that the machine is moving by itself, but the technician has programmed a computer that moves the machine to different spots.

The radiation session is easy. You come to the hospital, lie quietly on a table, and relax for a few minutes. If you need help staying still, your doctor has medicine that will help you. It is a wonderful feeling to know that each time you receive a treatment, you become healthier.

At some point during your radiation treatments, you may notice some changes in your body. These are called side effects. Side effects vary from person to person. Your doctor will explain what changes you might expect in your body.

Helpful Stories

The stories, **"Sparklers"** and **"Arcade Game"** help you visualize your body working with the radiation to stop unhealthy cells in your body.

Reread the **"Peaceful Swamp"** for a story about lying quietly on the treatment table.

SPARKLERS

"Radiation helps my healthy cells take charge."

Coaching Notes: *When you go for a radiation treatment, you can make up a story about watching fireworks. Thinking about this story will help you lie quietly and it will make the time go quickly. It will help you make a picture in your mind of unhealthy cells being destroyed. In this story you can use your imagination to think of sparklers in a way that helps you become healthier. Remember to always check with an adult before playing with real sparklers.*

Take time to relax your muscles and take calm, peaceful breaths. Use the following paragraph or another of your choice.

Close your eyes gently, or focus on a picture or a spot near you.

Take a few moments to remember the last time you were relaxed and how good it felt. When you are comfortable, take a nice, deep breath. Notice how the air fills your body.

As you breathe out, let peaceful feelings move throughout your body. Let the rhythm of music calm you. Feel your muscles relax and your heartbeat and breathing slow. Say to yourself: "I am calm and relaxed."

> Take three slow breaths and each time you breathe out, relax all your muscles.

Imagine that tonight is the night you have been waiting for all summer. It is the Fourth of July, and you are at the big celebration in town with rides, and music, and fireworks. The sun is starting to set. Soon it will be time for the fireworks to start. The sounds and lights of the carnival fade away as you walk with your family toward the big field where you will watch the fireworks.

When you find just the right spot, imagine spreading a blanket on the ground, and lying down to wait for the sunlight to fade from the sky. As you wait, notice people walking around you. You see someone eating pink cotton candy. The smell of popcorn fills the air. You hear children eagerly asking their parents when the fireworks will start. People are excited.

After awhile, the sky becomes dark enough and the show begins. Fireworks make loud cracking and sizzling sounds. They spray color across the dark sky. You shout and applaud for the big, beautiful displays.

In your imagination, pick up a sparkler that is lying on the ground beside you. Someone lights your sparkler for you. In the dark sky, your sparkling stick bursts with flashes of light. Hold the sparkler away from your body and swing it in circles to make patterns in front of you. You can make a happy face in the air, or a sad face, or a big round sun with sparks of energy radiating from it.

Now, make another picture in your mind. Imagine that you are at the hospital and you are getting ready to have a radiation treatment. Think about being on the treatment table, lying quietly. You are as comfortable and relaxed as you were when you imagined resting comfortably on a blanket at the park. Imagine that fireworks are about to begin, not outside in the sky, but inside your body. Technicians are walking around you adjusting your body for your treatment, and you think of them as the people walking around you at the park. You feel calm and relaxed as you get ready for your session.

As the treatment room darkens, imagine each of the healthy cells inside your body holding miniature sparklers just waiting to explode with energy. When you hear the radiation machine buzz, pretend the sparklers are lighting up and bursting with tiny flashes of heat. See your healthy cells waving sparklers around inside your body to locate any unhealthy cells in your body. The unhealthy cells are being damaged by the powerful bursts of light and heat. The hot bursts of twinkling lights target tiny cancer cells and destroy them. The damaged cells die and disappear. Your healthy cells fill in the space where the tumor had been growing. Repeat three times: **"Radiation helps my healthy cells take charge."** Each time the radiation machine buzzes, imagine more sparklers lighting the way to healing.

When your treatment is over, take a deep breath. As you breathe out, open your eyes. Use your imagination to think about a dark night sky filled with fireworks and then think about your body filled with healthy cells.

Each time you have a radiation treatment, it is a time for celebration. Celebrate as the unhealthy cells shrink away. You feel happy because you know that this is happening as you lie quietly during each session.

ARCADE GAME

"Unhealthy cells are easy targets."

Coaching Notes: *In this story, you will imagine playing an arcade game inside your body during radiation treatment sessions. You will visualize your body using your healthy cells to destroy disease. The unhealthy cells are easy targets because radiation weakens them.*

Take time to relax your muscles and take calm, peaceful breaths. Use the following paragraph or another of your choice.

Close your eyes gently, or focus on a picture or a spot near you.

Take a few moments to remember the last time you were relaxed and how good it felt. When you are comfortable, take a nice, deep breath. Notice how the air fills your body.

As you breathe out, let peaceful feelings move throughout your body. Let the rhythm of music calm you. Feel your muscles relax and your heartbeat and breathing slow. Say to yourself: "I am calm and relaxed."

Take three slow breaths and each time you breathe out, relax all your muscles.

I magine walking into a game arcade. You see bright lights flashing on all the different machines. Beeping and buzzing sounds fill the air. Kids are running from one game to the next. It is a place filled with movement and happiness.

As your eyes adjust to the dim lighting, look around and imagine walking past all the arcade games. You are anxious to start playing. You choose the game that uses a big padded mallet to hit objects when they pop out of holes. Drop a token into the machine.

As soon as the machine begins to buzz, you quickly grab a mallet. Objects start popping up all over the board. They are little animals, called moles, and only their heads peek out of the holes. You only have a few seconds to hit as many targets as possible.

Every few seconds an object pokes its head up somewhere on the game. You watch and aim carefully. You hit every one. You know how fast to move and you earn many points for smacking the targets. You are very good at this game!

Now, in your mind's eye take yourself to another place. Picture yourself at the hospital waiting for a radiation treatment. When you go into the treatment room, pretend you are going into a special arcade. While you lie completely still on the radiation table, picture your body filled with tiny little games like the one where you smash the objects that pop up. Imagine all of your healthy cells holding big padded mallet. Your healthy cells are going to pound away at the unhealthy cells. Your healthy cells use the power of the radiation x-rays to target the unhealthy cells and give them a big wallop that destroys their ability to move, just the way you are imagining the mallets bopping the objects in the arcade game.

Get ready for your treatment by saying to yourself: **"Unhealthy cells are easy targets."** Lie quietly and wait for the buzzing signal to start playing the game. Take a deep breath. Fill your lungs all the way to your stomach. Slowly let the air out. Now, take slow, even breaths and relax before the game begins.

BUZZ! Here it goes. Each time you hear the radiation machine buzz, pretend it is the signal that the games are starting. Cheer on your healthy, healing cells as they slam away at any sick cells in your body.

Your healthy cells are quick and strong. They can spot any cells that do not belong in your body. You hear another buzz and your body gets ready to play the game again. Your body uses the radiation to score big against sick cells. Repeat three times to yourself: **"Unhealthy cells are easy targets."**

When your radiation treatment is over, take a deep breath. As you breathe out, open your eyes. You feel relaxed and calm. During each radiation treatment your body wins more points against illness. When radiation damages a cancer cell it does not grow anymore. Hooray! More points for your healthy body.

STORIES TO HELP YOU FALL ASLEEP

215

> **Tips from Olivia, who wears a hearing device to help her hear**
>
> When you get ready for bed, have a book first and then look out the window and see if it is dark. Have your parents sing quiet songs to you. Think about being with your cousins and that they are saying special things to you.

Getting the right amount of sleep helps a person become healthier. When we fall asleep, lots of things are still happening in our bodies. During sleep, our bodies grow, do repair work, and slow down the work needed for digestion. All of this important work is going on and we don't even think about it, because we are sleeping!

For all of these reasons, it is important to get enough sleep. When we get the right amount of rest, we wake up refreshed. Of course, if we don't get enough sleep, our body works a double shift and we feel crabby and act cranky. We're tired out. We run out of energy.

When we are sick, our bodies need more rest and we tend to sleep quite a bit. Sometimes the medicines we take have a side effect of making us sleepy. Another reason for taking those extra naps is that our repair cells and immune cells are hard at work to make us healthy. That takes more energy, so we sleep more. Doesn't that make good sense? We send our energy to the places that need it.

Getting the right amount of rest is important. Once in awhile it is not easy to do. We sometimes have trouble falling asleep or staying asleep. It's a good idea to have a few plans to use when you want to relax and fall asleep.

YAWN! We have to sleep in a place we're not used to. There are noises that seem strange to us and it is hard to fall asleep.

TRY THIS: Bring your own pillow from home when you have to sleep in a new place. Bring along cuddly, comfortable pajamas, a blanket, or stuffed toy. Try using earplugs to block out some of the disturbing noises. Set a favorite picture on your table so you can look at it. All these things will help you relax and fall asleep.

YAWN! We have aches and pains and we have trouble finding a comfortable sleeping position. It's hard to ignore the hurt and be able to fall asleep.

TRY THIS: Imagine that you have a bottle of bubbles. Pretend to use your lips and your gentle breath to softly blow the imaginary bubbles. Watch them float above you. Breathe in a soft breath to fill your lungs and stomach. Then gently blow out bubbles and imagine them floating all around you. Try to picture funny animals inside each bubble. You can pretend there is a bubble circus entertaining you. When the show is over, you will be comfortable and will be able to fall asleep.

YAWN! Sometimes we're so bored from being in bed all day long. Day and night might get all mixed up and it is hard to feel tired enough to fall asleep.

TRY THIS: If at all possible, get out of your room for awhile. Walk the halls, go into the activity room, or visit the nurses' station. Even if you turn off TV and do something different, it will help. It is important to stretch all the muscles you can. Tense and release your muscles. Give yourself a mini-workout in your bed. Use progressive muscle relaxation and say the words, "calm and relax." Your body will be ready for rest.

YAWN! We're worried and our minds are filled with questions and concerns. It's difficult to clear our heads and relax so that we can fall asleep.

TRY THIS: Pretend that you are making a long distance phone call to someone who can listen to your worries. You have a phone card that is good for ten minutes. Make your imaginary phone call. Talk about all the things you are worried about. You say as much as you can in ten minutes, and then the card runs out. Hang up the phone and rest knowing that you have said all the things that are on your mind.

YAWN! We are staying in the hospital and people check on us all through the night. Our sleep gets disturbed and it is hard to fall back asleep.

TRY THIS: Sometimes when this happens to me I use the time to think about people I care about and I say a little prayer for each one of them. I concentrate on each person and soon I fall asleep. Another thing to try is the old trick of "counting sheep." You focus on a picture in your mind of something being slowly repeated over and over. Some people think about sheep jumping over a fence one by one. Doing this clears your mind so you can fall asleep.

YAWN! We have a dream that seems so real it wakes us up. We keep thinking about the dream and it is hard to go back to sleep.

TRY THIS: Look all around your room and say good night to each of the things in your room. You may have read a children's book that uses this same idea. By the time you get all the way around your room, your dream will not seem so important. Be sure not to watch scary shows or read scary stories before you go to bed.

Helpful Stories

Losing sleep is a problem that happens to all of us once in awhile. It's good to have several plans that you can use if it ever happens to you.

The stories **"Dream On"** and **"Pleasant Dreams"** will give you ideas for relaxing and falling asleep.

DREAM ON

"I dream happy dreams."

Coaching Notes: *In this story, you are encouraged to take time to focus on the positive aspects of each day to help you relax and feel ready for sleep.*

Take time to relax your muscles and take calm, peaceful breaths. Use the following paragraph or another of your choice.

Close your eyes gently, or focus on a picture or a spot near you.

Take a few moments to remember the last time you were relaxed and how good it felt. When you are comfortable, take a nice, deep breath. Notice how the air fills your body.

As you breathe out, let peaceful feelings move throughout your body. Let the rhythm of music calm you. Feel your muscles relax and your heartbeat and breathing slow. Say to yourself: "I am calm and relaxed."

Take three slow breaths and each time you breathe out, relax all your muscles.

Breathe slowly. The light is dim and you are getting ready to rest. In your imagination, climb onto a soft bed and lay down. The mattress gently hugs your entire body. Feel your toes, feet, legs, seat, back, arms, and hands relax as they sink into the mattress. Your head rests on a large, fluffy, feather pillow. Feel the tension leave your shoulders, neck and head as they sink into the pillow. You take relaxing breaths and as you breathe out, your body feels heavy with relaxation.

Reach down and pull the sheet up over your legs, your stomach, and up to your shoulders. Feel its cool softness relax the front of your body. Take a deep breath and smell the freshly washed sheet. It reminds you of a spring breeze. With the soft mattress on the bottom and the light sheet on top, you become a sandwich of relaxation. You are calm and relaxed.

Look out the open window next to your bed. The glow of moonlight in your room creates soft swirling shadows that dance across the ceiling. The soft sound of crickets chirping comes through your open window. In the distance, you hear the low sound of a train traveling across the countryside. The soft sounds of the evening help you relax even more deeply.

Look into the evening sky and notice the twinkling of the stars. As you watch the stars, see a picture of something good that happened to you today. Enjoy this scene.

Take a deep breath, blink, and see a picture of something nice you did for someone else. Enjoy this scene. These pictures stay in your mind as your eyes become heavy and begin to close. You are comfortable and at peace. As you fall asleep for the night, repeat to yourself three times, **"I dream happy dreams."**

Whenever you want to relax before you go to sleep, imagine the happy pictures that the stars make for you. When you look at them you see the good things that happened during your day.

PLEASANT DREAMS

"I go to sleep easily."

Coaching Notes: *This story provides a guided imagery relaxation exercise with a suggestion for using positive thinking before falling asleep.*

Take time to relax your muscles and take calm, peaceful breaths. Use the following paragraph or another of your choice.

Close your eyes gently, or focus on a picture or a spot near you.

Take a few moments to remember the last time you were relaxed and how good it felt. When you are comfortable, take a nice, deep breath. Notice how the air fills your body.

As you breathe out, let peaceful feelings move throughout your body. Let the rhythm of music calm you. Feel your muscles relax and your heartbeat and breathing slow. Say to yourself: "I am calm and relaxed."

Take three slow breaths and each time you breathe out, relax all your muscles.

It's been a busy day, but now it's time to get ready for bed. Imagine that you hear the doorbell ring. You walk to the door, open it, but find no one there. You look down and see a rectangular box lying on your front step. It is wrapped in paper that changes color before your eyes.

As you carry the package into the house, it feels warm and mysterious. Take a relaxing breath, and begin to untie the ribbons around the box. With an excited feeling, lift the lid off the box. Fold back the tissue paper, and see a pair of red slippers in your size and in the latest style.

Sit down, slip them on, and lean back to look at the slippers on your feet. Breathe in slowly and as you breathe out, your feet and legs begin to relax.

As you become more relaxed, the slippers begin to change color. Take another slow, easy breath. Concentrate on your feet and experience the feeling of relaxation. As you relax, the color of your slippers continues to change.

Breathe in and out slowly and deeply, and feel the tension completely leave your toes... feet... ankles... calves... knees... thighs. When your lower body is totally relaxed, your slippers will change into your favorite color.

Reach down, and lift the next layer of tissue paper from the box. Discover a beautiful robe, fit for a king or queen. As you hold it up in front of you, notice its beautiful color and design. The robe is woven from shiny golden thread.

Put one arm in the robe. You notice a feeling of security and comfort as your arm relaxes. Put the other arm in, and it too, relaxes. Your arms and hands and fingers become warm and your muscles seem to melt.

Take a breath and hold it. Put the magic robe over your shoulders. As you release your breath, button the gold buttons on the robe. The golden thread soaks up the light in the room and warms your arms,

223

shoulders, and chest. Enjoy the feeling, as your upper body is totally free of tension. You are calm and relaxed.

Reach down and find one more thing in the box. It is a beautiful, sparkling nightcap shaped like a cone. Put the hat on your head. This hat lets your mind relax and funnels into your head only happy, peaceful thoughts. There are so many good things about yourself to think about. Take a moment to think about one good thing about yourself.

Now it's time to turn off the light and go to sleep. Breathe slowly and easily in and out. Say to yourself three times: **"I go to sleep easily at night."** Take a relaxing breath and slowly let it out.

The person who left the magic clothes by your door wanted to tell you that you could feel comfortable and sleepy when it is time to go to sleep.

E ach night before you go to bed, look at your robe or pajamas, and think about one good thing about yourself. You go to sleep with positive thoughts and sleep well and wake up refreshed. Take a few moments to appreciate the good feelings that come with relaxation.

THINKING ABOUT YOUR FRIENDS

> **Tips from Caitlin, who was treated for epilepsy**
>
> I remember it was cool to meet an older girl with the same seizure disorder I have. She and I compared seizures and laughed with each other. I didn't feel so dumb then.

You might meet other children in the hospital or clinic that have the same illness you do. You'll be able to talk about the things you have in common and you'll find out that you are able to understand the things happening in each other's lives. You can make new friends.

As you and your friends compare notes, keep in mind that even though two people have the same illness, no two people have the same symptoms or the same rate of healing. Each person is unique. That means each person responds in his or her own way to treatments. Be sure to ask your parent or nurse if you have any questions or concerns about differences between you and a friend.

Explaining an Illness

While you are making new friends, your old friends are important, too. If you miss school because of sickness, your friends may wonder what is happening to you. There are many reasons that might cause a person to be sick, to be in the hospital, and to need some time away from school. If your friends understand something about what you are experiencing, it can help all of you feel more comfortable.

You may be wondering how to explain your disease to your friends. Parents, nurses, a teacher, counselor, or other special person can help you decide how to explain things. Many times you can find a book that talks about childhood diseases and can give you ideas. At the back of this book, there is a list of the titles of some books that may be helpful to you.

The Choice is Yours

It is your choice whom you tell and what details you tell them. When I tell people that I have cancer, some people remember someone else who had cancer. But illness affects different people in different ways, so my illness might be nothing at all like the other person they know who had cancer. It can be confusing.

You might be surprised at people's reactions. Some people need more time to think things over before they are ready to talk with you. When I told my friends that I had cancer, some of them did not know what to say to me. Other friends knew just what to say and helped me feel free to talk about my feelings.

Having a serious illness is a serious thing. Your friends need to know that your illness is treatable and that you are receiving the best possible treatment.

Be sure to tell your friends that you are not contagious; you do not have germs that they will catch. That means they will not get sick if they visit you or play with you.

You may want to tell your friends the name of your illness and then tell a couple of things about the way that it is affecting you. For example, "I don't have any hair right now because I'm taking a strong medicine and a side effect is that it makes hair fall out and stop growing. When I stop taking the medicine, my hair will grow back." Then give your friends a chance to ask questions. After that, your friends will probably have an idea of something else to talk about, or you might suggest playing something together.

How to Make Plans When You Don't Know How You'll Be Feeling

If a friend comes to visit, it would be nice to do something fun together. When you are healing from an illness, there are days when you feel great and then there are days when you don't feel so great. Often, you don't know ahead of time what kind of day is in store for you.

You can do many fun things with your friends even while you are lying in bed. If you will be resting at the hospital or at home for a few days, ask someone to help you gather some stuff to keep handy for when you want to play. Do something each day that is fun.

227

These ideas are just a few of the things you can enjoy with a friend.

card games   board games   puzzles   puppets
modeling clay   Legos   joke books   staring contest
music   coloring   watching TV/movies
Blowing bubbles and trying to catch them on your nose

What are your favorite things to do while resting in the hospital or at home?

Make a list of the ones you can do when you are alone and some that you can share with a friend. If you need to gather any special games or supplies for projects, ask someone to help you collect the things so that you have them handy for the times you want to use them.

_____

_____

_____

_____

_____

_____

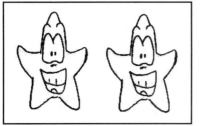

JOKES & RIDDLES

On days when quiet activities are best, many people enjoy working on a collection of some kind. One of the best collections a person can have is a collection that brings a smile to your face and creates a happy feeling — like a collection of jokes and riddles! Even in the midst of times that may seem scary and sad, it is possible for us to look for happiness.

When you have a collection of jokes, you have something you can always share with another person. Try out these jokes on your friends. Ask people to help you add to your collection!

"What house weighs the least?"

"A lighthouse."

Barb: "Do you think you can catch my cold?"

Gregg: "I don't know. How fast does it run?"

David: "My mother is in the hospital."

Sally: "That's too bad."

David: " No, it's not. She's a doctor."

Jo: "Knock, knock."

Jay: "Who's there?"

Jo: "Rhoda."

Jay: "Rhoda who?"

Jo: "Rhoda horse and fell off."

Barbie: "Why did the coach go into the bank?"

Jerry: " Because he wanted to get his quarter back."

Patient: "How can I avoid that run-down feeling?"

Doctor: "Look both ways before crossing the street."

"Why did the bee go to the doctor?"

"It had hives."

"What do you have when you drop your lollipop on the beach?"

"Sandy candy."

Ryan: "Where do you take a sick horse?"

Brenna: "To the horsepital."

230

SMILE AWHILE

Start collecting jokes, riddles, and comics that bring a smile to your face. Add them to these pages and share them with your friends.

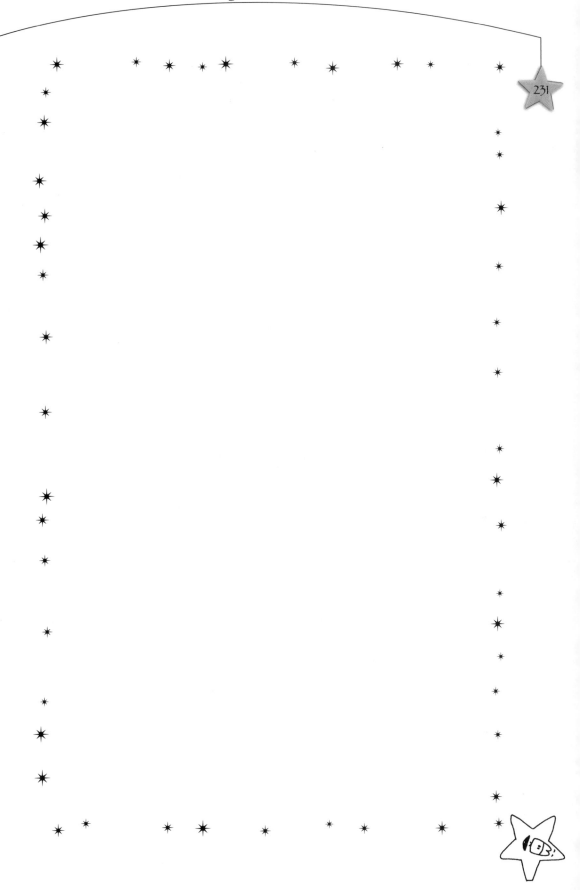

Dear Friend,
We certainly have gone on interesting adventures together... and we don't have to stop here. We can travel to many new places.
All you have to do is use your imagination. You can think of as many new stories as there are stars in the sky — or starfish in the sea.

Take care!
Love,
K. C.

GLOSSARY FOR CHILDREN

Many of the words that are used in medical settings may be new to you. Here are some of the words you may hear or read. Be sure to ask your coach and someone from your health care team if you have questions about any new words. Sometimes a new word sounds like another word that you already know, but its meaning is very different. If you are unsure of a meaning, ask for information.

Active Imagination: Using your imagination to see pictures or stories in your mind.

Anesthetic: A substance used to make a patient unconscious, or have no feeling of pain in preparation for surgery or certain medical tests or treatments.

> A *local anesthetic* numbs a specific area of the body. It may be given as a cream or by needle to cause a loss of feeling around that area only. Emla Cream is a lidocane-based cream that provides local anesthesia for needle sticks.

> A *general anesthetic* affects the whole body. It may be given by breathing it or by needle to cause the patient to go to "sleep" for an operation or other procedure. It may also be referred to as sedation medication.

Benign: Cells that are non-cancerous. They do not spread to other parts of the body or invade other tissue.

Biopsy: A procedure in which cells are removed from the body and examined under the microscope to tell if there have been any changes to the cells.

Blast Cells: A short name for **lymphoblast**, an immature white blood cell. In leukemia, blasts remain immature and accumulate in the bone marrow and crowd out the normal cells.

Bone Marrow: The soft tissue in the center of bones where blood cells are made.

Catheter: *(See Central Venous Access Line)* A plastic tube, which is inserted into the body, such as in a vein or the bladder. It is used to add or remove fluid from the body.

CAT Scan (or CT Scan): *Computerized Axial Tomography* is a diagnostic X-ray procedure that is used to detect masses in the body. A computer is used to generate a three-dimensional image of hard or soft tissue in the body. The machine has a round opening that looks like a giant doughnut surrounding a table.

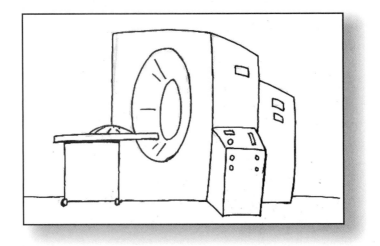

CBC (Complete Blood Count): A series of tests to examine the different parts of a person's blood. The tests are useful in diagnosing certain health problems and in following the results of treatment.

Cell: The basic structural unit of all living things. Each of the body's tissues is composed of many different types of cells. Cells are tiny and can be seen using a microscope. The cells in our body divide and multiply as needed.

235

Central Venous Access Line (CVL): A long catheter that is inserted into a large vein and can stay in place for an extended period of time. When it is used to give drugs or to take blood samples, an injection or finger stick is not needed. *External lines* (e.g. Broviac, Groshong, Hickman, PICC) are outside the skin while *internal lines* (e.g. Port-a-Cath) are under the skin. The device makes it easier to administer medicines such as chemotherapy.

Chemotherapy: The treatment of illness that uses drugs that are capable of interfering with the way cells divide. It is used to stop the growth of cancer cells. Although chemotherapy (sometimes called chemo) affects all cells, normal cells are better able to repair themselves than cancer cells.

Diagnosis: A doctor's opinion of what is causing a patient's problem, usually based on diagnostic tests and observations.

Distraction: Methods of diverting your attention away from uncomfortable feelings towards positive thoughts or activities to help reduce the feelings of pain and nervousness.

Finger Stick: When a finger stick is used to take a blood sample, a small prick is made in a finger and a few drops of blood are squeezed out.

Immunity: The power that a living organism has to resist and overcome infection. The immune system is the body's natural defense against disease producing substances. It is composed of white blood cells and antibodies that react against and fight off bacteria, viruses, and other organisms.

Infection: The invasion and multiplication of organisms that can make a person sick.

Injection: Usually known as a shot. An injection can be administered *IM* (intramuscular, usually in the leg or buttock), *IT* (intrathecal — spinal area), *IV* (vein), and *SC* (subq — subcutaneous, just under the skin.)

Leukemia: A type of cancer cell of the blood-forming tissues (bone marrow, lymph nodes, spleen) that multiplies in the blood stream and crowds out normal blood cells.

Lumbar Puncture (also called a Spinal Tap or LP): A technique for removing a small amount of the fluid that surrounds the brain and spinal cord. The fluid can be examined for changes in the cells and used for diagnostic purposes.

Lymphocyte: White blood cells that help a person stay healthy by destroying unwanted cells, such as cancer cells and germs.

Magnetic Resonance Imaging (MRI): A diagnostic procedure that uses magnetic fields and radio waves to produce pictures of internal parts of the body.

Malignant: A way of describing a cancerous tumor that may invade other tissues, spread to other parts of the body, or have the ability to destroy normal tissue.

Metastases: The spread of cancer cells from the original site to another place in the body.

Oncology: The branch of medicine that deals with cancer, including its causes and treatment.

Plasma: The liquid portion of the blood in which the cells and elements are suspended. It contains numerous proteins and minerals necessary for normal body functioning.

Platelet: The job of platelets is to help stop the bleeding if a person gets cut. Platelets are the part of blood that makes it clump (clot) together. If the platelet count is low, a person should be protected from injuries, because with fewer platelets, the person might bleed or bruise more easily. This might affect the type of games you are allowed to play in order to avoid bumps and bruises.

Positive Statements: The optimistic thoughts a person has about a situation, event, or themselves.

Progressive Muscle Relaxation (PMR): A method of decreasing pain, tension, and nervousness by focusing attention on relaxation of the muscles throughout the body.

Radiation Therapy: A form of treatment that uses high-energy rays to destroy cancer cells. Radiation can be administered externally (a radiation beam is delivered from a distance) or internally (by implanting radioactive isotopes within the tumor.)

Red Blood Cells: The job of red blood cells is to carry oxygen from the lungs to all the tissues in the body. All of our cells need oxygen. A low red blood cell count may mean a person will feel extra tired because there are fewer red blood cells to do the job of getting oxygen to your body parts. A person with a low red blood count may want to get extra rest.

Recurrence or Relapse: The reappearance of disease after treatment when symptoms had decreased or stopped.

Remission: The partial or complete disappearance, or the lessening of the severity of the disease.

Scan: A diagnostic procedure in which pictures of an organ or part of the body are obtained by using x-rays or radioactivity.

Stress: When a force (called a stressor) is exerted on a person and causes a physical or emotional change. The way a person feels about such an event contributes to how much stress one experiences.

Tumor: A growth or lump caused by cells growing in an abnormal way. A tumor can be benign or malignant.

Ultrasound Studies: A diagnostic procedure in which pictures are made by bouncing sound waves off organs to create an image of that tissue.

White Blood Cells (also leukocytes): The job of the white blood cells is to fight infection. They protect your body from enemies such as germs. If a white blood cell count is low, it is important to be protected from disease. Sometimes a child can wear a mask over his or her mouth and nose for extra protection from germs or infections while the white blood count is low.

X-Rays: Using radiant energy at low doses to diagnose disease and at high doses to treat disease.

Are you wondering about other words? Write any other new or confusing words in this space. Ask a member of your health care team to help you understand what the words mean.

_____

_____

_____

_____

_____

_____

_____

_____

_____

APPENDIX 1

Story Titles, Positive Statements, and Coaching Notes

The following list includes the title of each story with its Positive Statement and Coaching Notes.

Aquarium *(p. 110)*   **"My day is filled with interesting people."**

Coaching Notes: As you enter the hospital or your doctor's office, you often see people of all ages and sizes walking around or sitting in chairs waiting for their appointment. When you look around the waiting room, what do you notice? Do you see large glass windows? Do you see potted plants? Are there people moving about?

Use your imagination to think about going to a medical appointment. Pretend the office is really a large aquarium and the people are brightly colored tropical fish. Using your imagination helps you have calm thoughts as you wait for a treatment or for an appointment.

Arcade Game *(p. 212)*   **"Unhealthy cells are easy targets."**

Coaching Notes: In this story, you will imagine playing an arcade game inside your body during radiation treatment sessions. You will visualize your body using your healthy cells to destroy disease. Unhealthy cells are easy targets because radiation weakens them.

Blast-Off! *(p. 116)*   **"My stomach stays calm and steady."**

Coaching Notes: Sometimes stomachs feel queasy on the trip to a medical appointment even before reaching the hospital or doctor's office. In this story, pretend to get ready for your appointment the way an astronaut gets ready for a launch. You can think about this story as you travel to your own appointments. The images in this story may be especially helpful before a chemotherapy appointment.

Candles *(p. 153)*   **"I breathe in comfort and peace.
I blow out difficulties and problems."**

Coaching Notes: In this story, a breathing exercise is explained by imagining blowing out a candle with brief bursts of air. This type of breathing can help you if you experience sharp pain.

Chalk Drawing *(p. 190)* **"Each day of treatment helps me become healthy."**

Coaching Notes: In this story, you will make a picture in your mind of your body washing away germs or unhealthy cells the way rain washes away a chalk drawing on the sidewalk.

Dolphins *(p. 146)* **"I can go to a calm, pain free place."**

Coaching Notes: Previous stories used the image of rising to sunshine to ease discomfort. Sometimes an opposite image works better. For example, a severe headache or fever may make a person want to find a dim, cool, quiet spot. In this story, a dolphin will guide you through cool water to help you find a place to relax. The images in this story may help you prepare for anesthesia or for procedures requiring sedation medication.

A Dragon *(p. 94)* **"It feels good to express my feelings."**

Coaching Notes: In this story, a dragon helps you express any of your feelings from anger to happiness. You are encouraged to express feelings in ways that are safe and that help you feel better.

Dream On *(p. 219)* **"I dream happy dreams."**

Coaching Notes: In this story you are encouraged to take time to focus on the positive aspects of each day to help you relax and feel ready for sleep.

A Flag *(p. 156)* **"I am happy, healthy, and strong."**

Coaching Notes: In this story, you locate a spot inside your body that is painful or uncomfortable. You use your imagination to mark the spot with a flag. You focus your attention only on the movement of the flag and are distracted from the uncomfortable feeling.

Field of Flowers *(p. 150)* **"I am able to make myself feel comfortable."**

Coaching Notes: Sometimes part of you hurts and you feel pain. Sometimes you need a treatment or a medical test that is uncomfortable. You cannot avoid the treatment but you can change the way it feels to you. It is possible to lessen uncomfortable sensations by using your imagination to focus on other feelings. In this story you will learn a way to change painful or uncomfortable feelings so they seem smaller to you.

The Giraffe *(p. 166)* **"My breathing settles my stomach."**

Coaching Notes: In this story you will focus on a rhythmic breathing pattern to help your stomach feel more comfortable. Then you will imagine a giraffe eating special mint leaves that soothe its stomach.

Hot Air Balloon *(p. 138)*   **"My body feels comfortable and at peace."**

Coaching Notes: In this story, a ride in a hot air balloon encourages you to rise above sensations of pain or discomfort. You will take an imaginary trip in your very own hot air balloon and you will think about being high above any problems or worries. Uncomfortable feelings will sink away.

The Lake *(p. 46)*   **"I feel supported and filled with hope."**

Coaching Notes: You may be feeling like you are always rushing: from one appointment to the next, to the hospital, to your home, to your work. In this story you steer your car off your regular route and take time to express some of the emotions you are feeling.

Paintbrush *(p. 135)*   **"I can brush away pain."**

Coaching Notes: Your skin is made up of billions of cells. You send messages to your brain through your skin cells. In this story you can use a real paintbrush to stimulate the skin as a way to distract yourself from uncomfortable sensations in your body. If a paintbrush is not available, use your fingertips or a textured fabric. Adapt the story for the approach that you are using. This story may be especially helpful to feel calm while you wait for medication to take effect.

Peaceful Swamp *(p. 120)*   **"I am comfortable, as I lie quiet and still."**

Coaching Notes: This is a story to help you lie quiet and still during your diagnostic scans or radiation treatments. During tests or radiation treatments you can use your imagination and pretend to be a peaceful alligator. Think about your quiet, peaceful body lying on the treatment or radiation table, just as an alligator lies quietly in a swamp.

Pleasant Dreams *(p. 221)*   **"I go to sleep easily."**

Coaching Notes: This story provides an guided imagery relaxation exercise with a suggestion for using positive thinking before falling asleep.

Putting Out Fires *(p. 183)*   **"The medicine I take helps my body heal."**

Coaching Notes: In this story, you imagine being a firefighter who puts out a fire by spraying water onto it. The idea is compared to the effects of medicine helping to eliminate disease. You will imagine that the medicine you take is putting out the "fires" (unhealthy cells) in your body.

Rainbows *(p. 176)* **"The medicine I take brightens my body with healing."**
Coaching Notes: Doctors prescribe medicine to fight disease and to calm pain. In this story, imagine some of your favorite flavors that match the colors of the rainbow. Think about swallowing these delicious tastes to make a rainbow in your stomach. Keep your rainbow in your mind when you take your medicine.

Remote Control *(p. 90)* **"I can create peaceful, happy and relaxed feelings."**
Coaching Notes: Each of us has a wide range of emotions and throughout the day our moods change. There are times in our lives when we can help ourselves feel better by changing how we feel about something. In this story, you will pretend to use a remote control, not for your TV, but for your emotions.

Sand Sieve *(p. 198)* **"I am filled with healthy cells."**
Coaching Notes: You can make pictures in your mind of your body getting healthy. In this story, a sand sieve is used as an image of the body ridding itself of unhealthy cells. The healing cells in the body are separated from the unhealthy cells in an effort to rid illness from the body.

The Settlers *(p. 162)* **"As I relax, my stomach settles down."**
Coaching Notes: Years ago, people rode in covered wagons and traveled over long, bumpy trails to settle in the west. In this story, you are taking a journey toward health with cues to settle an upset stomach.

Ship Deck *(p. 113)* **"I feel confident and calm in new experiences and new places."**
Coaching Notes: A visit to a hospital may be a new experience where you encounter new sights, sounds and smells. You may wonder what brings all the people to the hospital. On your trip to the hospital, you can use your imagination to create a story about taking a voyage on an ocean liner.

The Slide *(p. 142)* **"I climb up to good feelings."**
Coaching Notes: You can use this story to feel more comfortable and to rise above painful sensations

Snowflakes *(p. 180)* **"Healing is happening inside my body."**
Coaching Notes: This story gives you a way to think about the healing that is occurring inside your body. You can use your imagination to compare the snowflakes to the way your immune system gets help from the medicine you take to become healthier.

Soccer Victory *(p. 186)*

"My whole body works to help me be strong and healthy."

Coaching Notes: In this story, you will think about the healthy cells in your body working together as teammates to be winners against disease. Drops of medicine are compared to soccer balls. You will make a picture in your mind of kicking the medicine into the goal to defeat disease. You will see yourself surrounded by a strong team whenever you take medicine or chemotherapy. When your team scores you feel excited.

Sparklers *(p. 209)*

"Radiation helps my healthy cells take charge."

Coaching Notes: When you go for a radiation treatment, you can make up a story about watching fireworks. Thinking about this story will help you lie quietly and it will make the time go quickly. It will help you make a picture in your mind of unhealthy cells being destroyed. In this story you can use your imagination to think of sparklers in a way that helps you become healthier. Remember to always check with an adult before using a real sparkler.

A Tree *(p. 202)*

"My body changes and I am still me."

Coaching Notes: In this story, you will use an image of a tree to give you a picture of strength that you can use whenever you wish to be strong. Sometimes a serious illness or a medication can have side effects that cause our bodies to change. This story helps remind us that even with changes in our appearance, we are still the people we were before.

A Turtle *(p. 86)*

"I am strong and I have energy to enjoy my day."

Coaching Notes: In this story, a turtle leads you through progressive muscle relaxation, then suggests that your energy levels may be different at different times: times when you have little energy, or times when you feel fully rested and energetic. There will be suggestions to tighten your muscles. It is fine to imagine tightening any muscles that are difficult or painful to actually tighten. The images in this story may be especially helpful before bedtime or naps, anesthesia or sedation, or any time that you would like to feel relaxed.

APPENDIX 2

Cross Reference Guide to Major Topics

	Relaxing Your Muscles	Expressing Healing Messages	Calming Your Stomach	Feeling Confident and Calm	Taking Medicine	Decreasing Painful Sensations	Expressing Emotions	Preparing for Procedures
Aquarium	•			•				•
Arcade Game		•						•
Blast Off		•	•	•				•
Candles				•		•		
Chalk Drawing		•			•			
Dolphins	•	•		•		•		
Dragon	•			•			•	
Dream On	•			•				
Giraffe			•		•	•		
Field of Flowers		•		•				
A Flag			•			•		
Hot Air Balloon	•					•	•	
Paintbrush	•		•			•		
Peaceful Swamp	•			•				•
Pleasant Dreams	•			•				
Putting Out Fires		•			•			•
Rainbows		•			•			
Remote Control	•		•					•
Sand Sieve		•						•
The Settlers			•	•				
Ship Deck	•		•	•				•
The Slide	•			•		•	•	
Snow Flakes	•	•						
Soccer Victory		•			•			•
Sparklers	•	•		•				•
Tree	•	•						•
Turtle	•			•			•	

APPENDIX 3

Annotated List of Books for Children

There are many wonderful books that reflect the experiences and emotions accompanying different illnesses. Check with your medical team, your library, and a bookstore for additional titles.

Bahr, Mary. *If Nathan Were Here.* Grand Rapids, MI: Eerdmans Publishing, 2000.

A young boy grieves the loss of his best friend and thinks about how things would be if he were still alive.

Baznik, Donna, and Jayne Sestak. *Becky's Story: A Book to Share.* Bethesda, MD: Association for the Care of Children's Health, 1981.

The feelings of a young child whose brother was in a serious accident are explored. Reassures the child that the mixed-feelings about what is happening are all right. Illustrations can be colored.

Bennett, Cherie. *Zink.* New York: Delacorte Press, 1999.

With the help of a trio of zebras from the Serengeti sixth-grader Becky faces her battle with leukemia, her family's fears for her, and the possibility she might die.

Berger, Melvin. *Ouch! A Book about Cuts, Scratches, and Scrapes.* New York: Scholastic Inc., 1991.

Focuses on the blood system in the healing process from a cut, including explanations of blood cells, fibrin and the blood's role in fighting infection.

Bergman, Thomas. *One Day at a Time: Children with Leukemia.* Milwaukee, WI: Gaerth Stevens Children's Books, 1998.

Follows the story of two children with leukemia as they are treated for their illness.

Canfield, J., M. Hansen, and I. Dunlap. *Chicken Soup for the Kid's Soul.* Deerfield Beach, FL: Health Communications, Inc., 1998.

A collection of short stories, anecdotes, poems, and cartoons which present a positive outlook on life.

Carter, Alden, and Siri Carter. *I'm Tougher Than Asthma.* Morton Grove, IL: Albert Whitman & Company, 1996.

A young girl describes what it is like to live with asthma, how this condition affects the body, some of the things that trigger an attack, and what can be done to avoid problems.

246

Clifford, Christine. *Our Family Has Cancer, Too!* Duluth, MN: Pfeifer-Hamilton Publishers, 1997.

When their mother is diagnosed with cancer, sixth grader Tim and his younger brother visit her in the hospital, learn about radiation and chemotherapy, and help with the chores at home.

Cole, Joanna, and Bruce Degen. *The Magic School Bus: Inside the Human Body.* New York: Scholastic, Inc., 1989.

A close-up look at how human bodies get energy from food. Focuses on the circulatory, nervous, and digestive systems. Discusses cells and the parts of blood cells.

_____. *The Magic School Bus: Inside Ralphie, A Book about Germs.* New York: Scholastic, Inc., 1995.

A close-up look at how germs travel through the bloodstream and make a person sick and how the body makes a person well again.

Crowe, Karen. *me and my marrow.* Deerfield, IL: Fujisawa Healthcare, Inc., 1999.

Offers explanations about what a bone marrow transplant is, how it is done, what treatments feel like, and ways to cope during difficult times.

Dolan, Eileen. *Winning Over Asthma.* Amherst, MA: Pedipress, Inc., 1992.

A picture book using the story of five-year-old Graham to present facts about asthma, emphasizing how, with family and physicians working together, childhood asthma can be controlled. Illustrations can be colored.

Driscoll-Beatty, Monica. *My Sister Rose Has Diabetes.* Santa Fe, NM: Health Press, 1997.

Describes the management of Type 1 diabetes; highlighting the issues of those without diabetes who sometimes feel forgotten in a family preoccupied with this chronic condition.

Dudley, Mark Edward. *Epilepsy.* Parsippany, NJ: Crestwood House, 1997.

Discusses the causes, diagnosis, and treatment of epilepsy, the types of seizures, and the challenges of living with the disease.

Elkins, Gary R. *My Doctor Does Hypnosis.* American Society of Clinical Hypnosis Press, 1997.

Explains clinical hypnosis and how it can be used to help people feel better about medical or psychological problems.

Gaes, Jason. *My Book for Kids with Cansur.* Aberdeen, SD: Melius Publishing, 1987.

An eight-year-old boy with cancer describes his experiences with diagnosis, treatment, hospitalizations, side effects, coping skills, death, and the future.

Gellman, Rabbi Marc, and Monsignor Thomas Hartman. *Lost & Found: A Kid's Book for Living Through Loss.* New York: Morrow Junior Books, 1999.

Different kinds of losses are introduced: losing possessions, competitions, health, trust, and the permanent loss because of death — along with suggestions for handling each.

Gelman, Rita Golden. *Body Battles.* New York: Scholastic Inc., 1992.

Focuses on the natural defense systems of the body against harmful substances. Explains the role of the immune system, mucus, cilia, earwax, skin, stomach acid and the brain.

Gold, John Coppersmith. *Cancer.* Parsippany, NJ: Crestwood House, 1997.

Presents the cause, effects, diagnosis, and present treatment of cancer as well as the promising research for more effective ways to treat the disease.

Gosselin, Kim. *Taking Diabetes to School.* Valley Park, MD: Jay Jo Books, 1998.

Offers insights into the day-to-day life of a child with the chronic illness of diabetes. This book is designed to be read aloud in the child's classroom. A short "quiz" is included as well as tips for teachers.

_____. *Taking Seizure Disorders to School.* Valley Park, MD: Jay Jo Books, 1998.

Describes the types of seizures and what can be done to treat them. This book is designed to be read aloud in the child's classroom. A short "quiz" is included as well as tips for teachers.

Helgaard, Marge. *When Someone Has a Very Serious Illness: Children Can Learn to Cope with Pain or Loss.* Minneapolis: Woodland Press, 1991.

Designed as an art process to help children learn some basic concepts of serious illness and provide an opportunity to learn about and express related feelings.

Howe, James, and Mel Warshaw. *The Hospital Book.* New York: Beech Tree, 1994.

A guide to a stay in the hospital discussing what happens there, the people one meets, what will hurt, and how one gets better and goes home.

Hugel, Kelly. *Young People and Chronic Illness: True Stories, Help, Hope.* Minneapolis: Free Spirit Publishing, Inc., 1998.

Presents true accounts of young people living with a chronic illness including how they have learned to cope and remain hopeful. Also includes strategies for living with a chronic medical problem. Particularly appropriate for older children and teens.

Krementz, Jill. *How It Feels to Fight for Your Life: The Inspiring Stories of Fourteen Children Who are Living with Chronic Illness.* New York: Simon & Schuster, 1991.

Candid interviews with children ranging in age from seven to sixteen with potentially life-destroying conditions.

Krishner, Trudy. *Kathy's Hats: A Story of Hope.* Morton Grove, IL: Albert Whitman & Co., 1992.

Kathy's love of hats comes in handy when the chemotherapy treatments she receives for her cancer make her hair fall out.

Krueger, David W. *What is a Feeling?* Seattle: Parenting Press, Inc., 1993.

Uses familiar situations to help children put words to their wide range of feelings. Encourages children to value feelings as special and real.

Krulik, Nancy E. *Don't Stress! How to Keep Life's Problems Little.* New York: Scholastic, Inc., 1998.

Brief bits of advice about life's tiny aggravations.

Kuklin, Susan. *When I See My Doctor.* New York: Bradbury Press, 1988.

A four-year-old describes his trip to the doctor for a physical examination. Photographs show the instruments used in the evaluation.

Mills, Joyce. *Little Tree, A Story for Children with Serious Medical Problems.* New York: Magination Press, 1992.

Although she is saddened that storm damage has caused her to lose some of her branches, Little Tree draws strength and happiness from the knowledge that she still has a strong trunk, deep roots, and a beautiful heart.

_____. *Gentle Willow, A Story for Children about Dying.* New York: Magination Press, 1993.

A story about a squirrel, Amanda, who is upset that she is going to lose her friend Gentle Willow, but the tree wizards help her understand that there are special ways of saying goodbye. Provides analogies to medical interventions.

Maple, Marilyn. *On the Wings of a Butterfly: A Story about Life and Death.* Seattle: Parenting Press, 1992.

A little girl with cancer meets a caterpillar preparing for transformation. The caterpillar loses her skin, paralleled to the girl losing her hair. The caterpillar turns into a chrysalis and feelings of fear are discussed. The little girl returns home to die, but not before seeing her friend turn into a butterfly.

Nessim, Susan, Barbara Wyman, and Susan Avishai. *A Friend for Life, A Story and Activity Book for Kids with Cancer.* Los Angeles: Cancervive, 1994.

A storybook and task-oriented activity book specifically designed for children with cancer ages 7 - 11.

Ostrow, William, and Vivian Ostrow. *All About Asthma.* Morton Grove, IL: Albert Whitman & Company, 1989.

The young narrator describes life as an asthmatic, explains causes and symptoms of asthma, and discusses ways to control the disorder and lead a normal life.

Payne, Lauren Murphy. *Just Because I Am: A Child's Book of Affirmation.* Minneapolis: Free Spirit Publishing, 1994.

Fourteen affirming statements, with appealing illustrations, about self-acceptance; supports a child's self-esteem.

Peacock, Carol. *Sugar Was My Best Friend: Diabetes and Me.* Morton Grove, IL: Albert Whitman & Co., 1998.

An eleven-year-old boy describes how he learned that he had diabetes, the effect of the disease on his life, and how he learned to cope with the changes in his life.

Peterkin, Alan. *What About Me? When Brothers & Sisters Get Sick.* New York: Magination Press, 1992.

A young girl experiences conflicting emotions when her brother becomes seriously ill. Includes suggestions for parents to help their well children cope with a chronically ill sibling.

Richter, Donna, and Kenneth Grofinkle. *When Brian Got Cancer.* New York: Memorial Sloan-Kettering Hospital, Division of Nursing, 1990.

A photo-essay focuses on a child's diagnosis and treatment in the hospital, including chemotherapy and surgery.

249

Rogers, Fred. *Going to the Hospital.* New York: Putnam & Grosset Group, 1997.
Describes what happened during a stay in the hospital, including some of the common forms of medical treatment.

Saltzman, David. *The Jester Lost His Jingle.* The Jester, Co. Inc.
Cancer patient David Saltzman wrote this fable about a jester who lost his trademark jingle and his journey to understand why. He meets a young girl with a brain tumor who is in pain and very sad, but he is able to make her laugh. The jester returns to the king and explains that laughter is inside of all of us. Ages 5 - 10.

Shapiro, Jan. *Diane Dino's Dilemma, A Story of von Willebrand Disease.* Collegeville, PA: Armour Pharmaceutical Company, 1994.
Informs and educates about the symptoms of von Willebrand disease, a disease where the blood is missing a factor involved in clotting.

Shriver, Maria. *What's Heaven?* New York: Golden Books. 1999.
After her grandmother's death, a young girl learns about heaven by asking her mother questions.

Siegler, Kathryn, Maxie Chambliss, and Renee Jablow. *I'm Going to the Doctor: A Pop-Up Book.* New York: Ladybird Books, 1997.
Introduces the common aspects of a doctor's appointment, including drawings of the instruments the doctor and nurse will likely use to examine the child. Appropriate for preschoolers.

Warner, Sally. *Sort of Forever.* New York: Alfred A. Knopf, Inc., 1998.
Twelve-year-olds Cady and Nana explore the strengths of their special friendship as they cope with Nana's cancer. The novel details changes that occur in both of the girls' lives.

Weil, Kelly. *Zink the Zebra, A Special Tale.* Milwaukee: Gareth Stevens Publishing, 1996.
A courageous spotted zebra is used as an insightful role model when discussing sensitive topics of human differences. Zink encourages feeling of compassion, understanding, and respect in young children. The author is a young girl who had cancer.

Wisconsin Cancer Pain Initiative. *Jeff Asks About Cancer Pain.* Madison, WI: University of Wisconsin Medical School, 1990.
Jeff, a teenager, is reassured that a diagnosis of cancer does not mean he will experience pain. Discusses various pain relief methods. Question and answer format.

Appendix 4

Organizations Offering Information and Resources

The following organizations are representative of the many resources available to you. Use your medical team and the World Wide Web to locate additional sources of information. Since email and www addresses change frequently, it is possible that the following addresses may need to be updated.

Make-A-Wish Foundation of America

2600 North Central Avenue, Suite 936
Phoenix, AZ 85004
(602) 240-6600
www.wish.org

This organization grants the wishes of children with life-threatening illnesses to enrich the human experience with hope, strength, and joy.

Ronald McDonald House (national headquarters)

Golin-Harris Communications, Inc
500 North Michigan Avenue
Chicago, IL 60611
(312) 836-7114
www.rmhc.com

RMDH Charities provides comfort and care to children and their families by supporting RMD Houses in communities around the world and making grants to other not-for-profit organizations whose programs help children.

Starbright Foundation

1990 S. Bundy Drive
Los Angeles, CA 90025
(310)442-1560
www.starbright.org

This organization is dedicated to the development of projects that empower seriously ill children by linking them to peers and to information that may help them better understand the challenges they face. Starbright Foundation is a nonprofit organization chaired by film director Steven Spielberg and retired Gen. Norman Schwarzkopf.

RESOURCES FOR SPECIFIC ILLNESSES

Asthma

Asthma & Allergy Foundation of America
1 (800) 7-ASTHMA
Fax: (202)-466-8940
www.aafa.org
Email: info@aafa.org

American Lung Association
1 (800) LUNG-USA (586-4872)
www.lungusa.org

National Asthma Education and Prevention Program
(301) 592-8573
Fax: (301) 592-8563
www.nhlbi.gov

Cancer

American Cancer Society
1 (800) ACS-2345
www.cancer.org

Candlelighters Childhood Cancer Foundation
1 (800) 366-2223
Fax: (301) 718-2686
www.candlelighters.org
Email: info@candlelighters.org

Leukemia and Lymphoma Society
1 (800) 955-4LSA
Fax: (212) 573-8484
www.leukemia.org
Email: infocenter@leukemia-lymphoma.org

National Cancer Institute
1 (800) 4CANCER (422-6237)
www.nci.nih.gov

National Childhood Cancer Foundation
1 (800) 458-NCCF
Fax: (626) 447-6459
www.nccf.org

Congenital Heart Defects

Kids with Heart: National Association for Children's Heart Disorders
1 (800) 538-5390
Fax: (920) 498-0058
www.execpc.com/~kdswhrt
Email: kdswhrt@execpc.com

Cystic Fibrosis

Cystic Fibrosis Foundation
1 (800) FIGHTCF (344-4823)
Fax: (301) 951-6378
www.cff.org/
Email: info@cff.org

Cystic Fibrosis Index of On-Line Resources
vmsb.csd.mu.edu/

Diabetes

American Diabetes Association
1 (800) DIABETES (342-2383)
Fax: (703) 549-6995
www.diabetes.org
Email: customerservice@diabetes.org

Children with Diabetes
www.kwd.org

Epilepsy

Epilepsy Foundation of America
1 (800) EFA-1000
Fax: (301) 577-2684
www.efa.org

American Epilepsy Society
(860) 586-7505
www.aesnet.org
Email: info@aesnet.org

Hemophilia

National Hemophilia Foundation
1 (800) 42-HANDI
Fax: (212) 328-3777
www.hemophilia.org
Email: info@hemophilia.org

Inflammatory Bowel Diseases

Crohn's and Colitis Foundation of America
1 (800) 932-2423
Fax: (212) 779-4098
www.ccfa.org
Email: info@ccfa.org

Juvenile Rheumatoid Arthritis

American Juvenile Arthritis Organization
(404) 872-7100, ext. 6227
Fax: (404) 872-0457
www.arthritis.org/ajao

Pediatric Rheumatology Home Page
www.goldscout.com

Kidney Disease

Polycystic Kidney Research Foundation
1 (800) PKD-CURE
Fax: (816) 931-8655
http://pediatrics.about.com
Email: pkdcure@pkrfoundation.org

Lupus

Lupus Foundation of America

1 (800) 558-0121

FAX: (301) 670-9486

www.internet-plaza.net/lupus/

Sickle Cell Disease

Sickle Cell Disease Association of America

1 (800) 421-8453

Fax: (310) 215-3722

www.sicklecelldisease.org

Email: scdaa@sicklecelldisease.org

HELPFUL WEB SITES

Healing Images

Offers information and support to parents with a child facing a serious illness. Research supporting the mind-body connection is referenced as well as a listing of helpful Web sites and books.

(920) 262-0439

Fax: (920) 261-8801

www.healingimages.net

Email: kids@readysetrelax.com

Inner Coaching

Provides resource information for anyone interested in the effects of stress in children. Several proven programs intended to reduce harmful stress, increase self-esteem, and decrease anxiety are outlined. Beneficial music selections, sample scripts, and relaxation exercises are provided.

(920) 262-0439

Fax: (920) 261-8801

www.innercoaching.com

Email: kids@readysetrelax.com

National Institutes of Health
www.nih.gov

The Never-Ending Squirrel Tale

Developed for parents of children with cancer. It includes personal stories from parents, an online newsletter, information, and resources. This is a visually and emotionally appealing site that is easy to navigate and is a valuable source of support and information for families.
www.squirreltales.com

Oncolink

An online center for cancer resources sponsored by the University of Pennsylvania. The site offers news, a substantial number of book reviews, "Editor's Choice Awards" given to worthwhile cancer related web sites, and a virtual gallery of art created by people whose lives have been touched by cancer.
www.oncoline.upenn.edu

Pediatrics Home Page

Site offering extensive index of links and information about hundreds of childhood diseases and child development issues.
www.pediatrics.about.com

Add additional resources that you have found to be helpful.

_____

_____

_____

_____

_____

_____

_____

_____

_____

_____

_____

APPENDIX 5

Healing Images for Children CD

The CD is available through Inner Coaching to provide you with ready access to the relaxation exercises and active imagination stories in this book.

- The progressive relaxation script and the stories on the CD can serve as a guide for the time needed for pacing and pausing during the stories when they are read aloud.

- The background music gives an idea of the type of calming music that enhances relaxation.

- The CD can be helpful to use as reinforcement after the child and coach have practiced a story together.

- The CD can be played in the car on your way to appointments or in waiting rooms to help your child become prepared for a treatment or therapy.

- The last track on the CD is a selection of peaceful, calming music without words. It can be played to elicit relaxation or can be used as background music when a relaxation exercise, or an active imagination story from the book, or one of your own is read aloud.

Track 1 Introduction

Track 2 Progressive Muscle Relaxation Exercise

"I am calm and relaxed."
Coaching Notes: In this exercise, you will learn to relax by tensing and then releasing the tension in your muscles. You will focus on the contrasting feelings of tension and relaxation. If there are restrictions on your ability to tense your muscles, it is fine for you to tighten those muscles only in your imagination. You will still gain benefit from imagining muscle tension.
Length: 20 minutes

Track 3 A Turtle

"I am strong and I have energy to enjoy my day."
Coaching Notes: In this story, a turtle leads you through progressive muscle relaxation, then suggests that your energy levels may be different at different times: times when you have little energy, or times when you feel fully rested and energetic. There will be suggestions to tighten your muscles. It is fine to imagine tightening any muscles that are difficult or painful to actually tighten. The images in this story may be especially helpful before bedtime or naps, anesthesia or sedation, or any time that you would like to feel relaxed.
Length: 9 minutes

Track 4 Ship Deck

"I feel confident and calm in new experiences and new places."

Coaching Notes: A visit to a hospital may be a new experience where you encounter new sights, sounds and smells. You may wonder what brings all the people to the hospital. On your trip to the hospital, you can use your imagination to create a story about taking a voyage on an ocean liner.

Length: 7 minutes

Track 5 Soccer Victory

"My whole body works to help me be strong and healthy."

Coaching Notes: In this story, you will think about the healthy cells in your body working together as teammates to be winners against disease. Drops of medicine are compared to soccer balls. You will make a picture in your mind of kicking the medicine into the goal to defeat disease. You will see yourself surrounded by a strong team whenever you take medicine or chemotherapy. When your team scores you feel excited.

Length: 7 minutes

Track 6 Hot Air Balloon

"My body feels comfortable and at peace."

Coaching Notes: In this story, a ride in a hot air balloon encourages you to rise above sensations of pain or discomfort. You will take an imaginary trip in your very own hot air balloon and you will think about being high above any problems or worries. Uncomfortable feelings will sink away.

Length: 9 minutes

Track 7 Dolphins

"I can go to a calm, pain free place."

Coaching Notes: Previous stories used the image of rising to sunshine to ease discomfort. Sometimes an opposite image works better. For example, a severe headache or fever may make a person want to find a dim, cool, quiet spot. In this story, a dolphin will guide you through cool water to help you find a place to relax. The images in this story may help you prepare for anesthesia or for procedures requiring sedation medication. The story ends without the suggestion to open the eyes and stretch. It allows the child to continue resting or fall asleep.

Length: 7 minutes

Track 8 Dream On

"I dream happy dreams."

Coaching Notes: In this story you are encouraged to take time to focus on the positive aspects of each day to help you relax and feel ready for sleep.

Length: 5 minutes

Track 9 music for relaxing (without words)

Length: 5 minutes

BIBLIOGRAPHY

Achterberg, Jeanne. *Imagery and Healing: Shamanism and Modern Medicine.* Boston: Shambhala Publications, 1985.

Adams, David W., and Eleanor J. Deveau. *Coping with Childhood Cancer — Where Do We Go From Here?* Hamilton, Ontario: Kinbridge Publications, 1988.

Albom, Mitch. *Tuesdays with Morrie.* New York: Doubleday, 1997.

Allen, Jeffrey, M.Ed., and Roger Klein Psy.D. *Ready, Set, R.E.L.A.X.: A Research Based Program of Relaxation, Learning and Self Esteem for Children.* Watertown, WI: Inner Coaching, 1996.

Benson, Herbert. *The Relaxation Response.* New York: Avon Books, 1975.

_____., and William Proctor. *Beyond the Relaxation Response.* New York: Berkeley, 1985.

Bolen, Jean Shinoda. *Close to the Bone: Life-Threatening Illness and the Search for Meaning.* New York: Touchstone, 1996.

Borysenko, Joan. *Minding the Body, Mending the Mind.* Massachusetts: Addison-Wesley, 1987.

Buchanan, Sue. *I'm Alive and the Doctor's Dead: Surviving Cancer with Your Sense of Humor Intact.* Grand Rapids, MI: Zondervan Publishing House, 1994.

Bush, Carol A. *Healing Imagery and Music: Pathways to the Inner Self.* Portland, OR: Rudra Press, 1995.

Clark, Elizabeth. *You Have the Right To Be Hopeful.* Silver Spring, MD: National Coalition for Cancer Survivorship, 1997.

Cousins, Norman. *Anatomy of an Illness.* New York: Bantam Books, 1979.

_____. *Head First: The Biology of Hope.* New York: E. P. Dutton, 1989.

DeMille, Richard. *Put Your Mother on the Ceiling: Children's Imaginative Games.* New York: Penguin Books, 1976.

Dilley, Ingrid, Carol Troestler, and Josiah Dilley. *Renewing Life.* Madison, WI: 1995.

Fromer, Margot Joan. *Surviving Childhood Cancer: A Guide For Families.* Oakland, CA: New Harbinger Publications, Inc., 1995.

Gorfinkle, Kenneth. *Soothing Your Child's Pain.* Lincolnwood, IL: Contemporary Books, 1998.

Grollman, Earl A. *Talking About Death: A Dialogue between Parent and Child.* Boston, MA: Beacon Press, 1990.

Hirshberg, Caryl, and Marc Ian Barasch. *Remarkable Recovery: What Extraordinary Healings Tell Us About Getting Well and Staying Well.* New York: Riverhead Books, 1995.

Humphrey, J.H., and J. N. Humphrey. *Stress in Childhood.* New York: AMS Press, Inc., 1984.

Hyde, Margaret O., and Lawrence Hyde. *Cancer in the Young: A Sense of Hope.* Philadelphia: Westminster Press, 1985.

Kabat-Zinn, Jon. *Full Catastrophe Living: Using the Wisdom of Your Body and Mind to Face Stress, Pain and Illness.* New York: Dell Publishing, 1990.

_____. *Wherever You Go, There You Are: Mindfulness Meditation in Everyday Life.* New York: Hyperion, 1994.

Keene, Nancy. *Childhood Cancer: A Parent Guide to Solid Tumor Cancers.* Sevastopol, CA: O'Reilly & Associates, 1999.

_____. *Childhood Leukemia: A Guide for Families, Friends & Caregivers.* Sevastopol, CA: O'Reilley & Associates.

Kushner, Harold. *When Bad Things Happen to Good People.* New York: Avon Books, 1983.

LeShan, Lawrence. *Cancer as a Turning Point.* New York: E. P. Dutton, 1989.

_____. *You Can Fight For Your Life: Emotional Factors in the Treatment of Cancer.* New York: M. Evans and Company, Inc., 1977.

Levine, Barbara Hoberman. *Your Body Believes Every Word You Say: The Language of the Body/Mind Connection.* Fairfield, CT: Aslan Publishing, 1991.

Moyers, Bill. *Healing and the Mind.* New York: Doubleday, 1993.

Myss, Caroline. *Anatomy of the Spirit: The Seven Stages of Power and Healing.* New York: Crown Publishers, Inc., 1996.

Nessim, Susan, and Ernest Katz, Ph.D. *Cancervive Teacher's Guide for Kids with Cancer.* Los Angeles: Cancervive, 1999.

Olness, Karen, M..D., and Gail G. Gardner, Ph.D. *Hypnosis and Hypnotherapy with Children*. Philadelphia, PA: Harcourt Brace Jovanovich, Inc., 1988.

Remen, Rachel Naomi, M.D. *Kitchen Table Wisdom: Stories that Heal*. New York: Riverhead Books, 1996.

Rolsky, Joan Taska. *Your Child Has Cancer: A Guide to Coping*. Philadelphia, PA: Committee to Benefit the Children, St. Christopher's Hospital, 1992.

Selyes, Hans. *The Physiology and Pathology of Exposure to Stress*. Montreal: Acta, 1950.

Siegel, Bernie, M.D. *Love, Medicine & Miracles: Lessons Learned About Self-Healing From a Surgeon's Experience with Exceptional Patients*. New York: HarperCollins, 1986.

_____. *How to Live Between Office Visits: A Guide to Life, Love and Health*. New York: HarperCollins, 1993.

Seligman, Martin P. *The Optimistic Child: A Proven Program to Safeguard Children Against Depression and Build Lifelong Resilience*. New York: HarperCollins, 1996.

Simon, David. *Return to Wholeness: Embracing Body, Mind, and Spirit in the Face of Cancer*. New York: John Wiley & Sons, 1999.

Simonton, O. Carl, Stephanie Matthews-Simonton, and James L Creighton. *Getting Well Again*. New York: Bantam Books, 1978.

Simonton, O. Carl, and Reid Henson. *The Healing Journey: The Simonton Center Program for Achieving Physical, Mental, and Spiritual Health*. New York: Bantam Books, 1992.

Stone, Bob, and Jenny Stone Humphries. *Where the Buffaloes Roam: Building a Team for Life's Challenges*. New York: Addison-Wesley Publishing Company, 1993.

Talking with Your Child about Cancer. Bethesda, MD: National Institutes of Health, 1988.

Wester, William C. Ed.D., and Donald J. O'Grady, Ph.D. *Clinical Hypnosis with Children*. New York: Brunner/Mazel, Inc., 1991.

Weil, Andrew. *Spontaneous Healing*. New York: Ballantine Books, 1995.

Young People and Cancer: A Handbook for Parents. Bethesda, MD: National Institutes of Health.

INDEX

NOTES

NOTES

267

ORDERING INFORMATION

HEALING IMAGES FOR CHILDREN:
Teaching Relaxation and Guided Imagery to Children Facing Cancer and Other Serious Illnesses
Written by Nancy C. Klein, M.A.

A comprehensive guide for parents, health care providers, and other caring individuals complete with educational information relating to medical treatments and relaxation strategies. The first section of the book is written for adults and provides background information on research describing the healing power of relaxation, music, imagery, and humor. The second section includes chapters designed specifically to help children develop coping strategies to reduce the pain and anxiety of medical procedures and treatments. Twenty-seven stories help children reframe the medical and emotional aspects of illness with positive statements that reinforce one's ability to cope with difficulties. The guide is beautifully illustrated. A valuable adjunct to traditional medical interventions.

240 pages / 7 x 10 Softcover / ISBN 0-9636027-2-1

HEALING IMAGES FOR CHILDREN CD
Written by Nancy C. Klein, Narrated by Roger Klein

Seven stories and a progressive muscle relaxation exercise are set to a background of calming music. The CD is a convenient, helpful way to reinforce the relaxation, breathing, and active imagination techniques from the book *Healing Images for Children*. It provides ready access to the calming messages from the book. Children can use the CD on the way to appointments, in waiting rooms, as well as during therapy.

70-minute audio recording / ISBN 0-9636027-3-X

HEALING IMAGES FOR CHILDREN ACTIVITY BOOK:
For Days When Quiet Activities are Best
Written by Nancy C. Klein, M.A., Illustrated by Matthew Holden

A playful puppy, named Bailey, encourages children to express themselves and make this book their own through the exciting activities in this interactive workbook. Coloring, drawing, playing, and writing activities reinforce the themes of the active imagination stories and the positive messages regarding confidence,

269

courage, and comfort. The individual activities are at several levels of difficulty appropriate for children ranging in age from 4 to 12 years old. The book gives a sense of peace and well being along with encouragement and self-help ideas for any child coping with illness and/or hospitalization.

90 pages / 8 x 11 Softcover / ISBN 0-9636027-4-8

HEALING IMAGES FOR CHILDREN RELAXATION KIT
Activities to Bring Comfort — Toys to Bring Joy
Guidebook Written by Nancy C. Klein, M.A.

Delightful activities chosen specifically to help a child remember the qualities from the active imagination stories in *Healing Images for Children*. Includes hands-on toys that can be tucked into a pocket and carried into waiting rooms, treatments, and diagnostic tests. Included are creative crafts, toys, stickers, and objects that stimulate personal interpretations of the stories and help children anchor their personal healing images. The components can be used therapeutically to encourage physical as well as emotional expression. All items are packaged in a vinyl carrying bag with handles. A guidebook with suggestions for use is included.

(Includes items not recommended for children under 3 years of age.) ISBN 0-9636027-5-6

HEALING IMAGES FOR CHILDREN NOTE CARDS

Eight blank cards each with a different picture representing a theme from an active imagination story in *Healing Images for Children*. The cards may be used as focal points to help children concentrate during difficult times or during relaxation exercises. Children may wish to write their own stories and positive messages inside the cards. The cards can be used to send encouragement to a loved one. (Includes envelopes)

RELAXATION AND SUCCESS IMAGERY

(Klein & Klein) — A progressive muscle relaxation exercise including positive self-statements. Suitable for teenagers and adults. Original guitar background music. Available on tape.

MUSIC FOR RELAXATION, LEARNING, AND THERAPY

Studies show that music can reduce pain, unlock creativity, ease depression, and improve behavior. The following tapes/CDs are recommended and available through Inner Coaching.

Pianoscapes (Michael Jones) — Soothing piano solos.

Language of Love (Gary Lamb) — Relaxing music for classrooms, offices, or hospitals.

Pachelbel w/Ocean (Liv & Let Liv) — Cannon in D soundscape with three variations.

Bach Forever by the Sea (Dan Gibson) —Ten classics with sounds of the sea.

The Fairy Ring (Mike Rowland) — Music for piano/synthesizer.

ADDITIONAL RESOURCES FROM INNER COACHING

READY...SET...R.E.L.A.X.

Written by Jeffrey S. Allen, M.Ed. and Roger J. Klein, Psy.D.

Beyond reviewing the causes of stress, this book equips children ages 5 to 13 years old with tools to overcome anxiety through the use of music, muscle relaxation, and storytelling to promote learning, imagination, and self-esteem. This fully researched program is used across the country by teachers, counselors, parents, and medical professionals as a preventive tool and intervention strategy. The 66 scripts focus on the following themes: **R**=Releasing Tension; **E**=Enjoying Life; **L**=Learning; **A**=Appreciating Others; **X**=X-panding Your Knowledge. Easy to use. Includes follow-up activities.

204 pages / 8.5 x 11 softcover / ISBN 0-9636027-0-5

READY...SET...RELEASE

Written by Jeffrey S. Allen, M.Ed. and Roger J. Klein, Psy.D.

This 74-minute cassette tape or audio CD offers 14 fun and calming exercises using music, breathing, muscle relaxation, and guided active imagination to soothe and release tension. This companion (or stand alone) piece to the book Ready...Set...R.E.L.A.X. has proven effective for children from preschool to middle school.

ISBN 0-9636027-1-3

Specializing in products and activities that foster positive thinking, reduce stress and build self-esteem in children.
www.innercoaching.com

ORDER FORM

To order any of the resources listed below fill out this form and fax purchase order to (920) 261-8801, or mail check and order form to:

Inner Coaching, 1108 Western Avenue, Watertown, WI 53094

QTY.	ITEM	PRICE	TOTAL
_____	Healing Images for Children	$24.95	_____
_____	Healing Images for Children CD	$15.95	_____
_____	Healing Images Activity Book	$12.95	_____
_____	*Special package: above 3 items*	*$47.95*	_____
_____	Healing Images Relaxation Kit	$29.95	_____
_____	Healing Images Note Cards	$12.00	_____
_____	Ready...Set...R.E.L.A.X.	$23.95	_____
_____	Ready, Set, Release tape/CD	$10.95/15.95	_____
_____	Relaxation & Success Imagery	$10.95	_____

MUSIC SELECTIONS

Tape / CD

_____	*Pianoscapes* (Michael Jones)	$10.95/15.95	_____
_____	*Language of Love* (Gary Lamb)	$10.95/15.95	_____
_____	*Pachelbel w/Ocean* (Liv & Let Liv)	$10.95/15.95	_____
_____	*Bach Forever by the Sea* (D. Gibson)	$10.95/15.95	_____
_____	*The Fairy Ring* (Mike Rowland)	$10.95/15.95	_____

*Add $3.50 for first item and $.50 each additional item. **SHIPPING*** _____

WI Residents add: 5.5% **Sales Tax** _____

TOTAL _____

Orders must be accompanied by check or money order made payable to Inner Coaching. Guaranteed — return within 30 days for refund if dissatisfied.

SHIP TO:

Name: _____

Address: _____

Phone: _____

E-Mail: _____

(This information will not be released to others.)

Please use Order Form on reverse

ORDER FORM

To order any of the resources listed below fill out this form and fax purchase order to (920) 261-8801, or mail check and order form to:

Inner Coaching, 1108 Western Avenue, Watertown, WI 53094

QTY.	ITEM	PRICE	TOTAL
_____	Healing Images for Children	$24.95	_____
_____	Healing Images for Children CD	$15.95	_____
_____	Healing Images Activity Book	$12.95	_____
_____	*Special package: above 3 items*	*$47.95*	_____
_____	Healing Images Relaxation Kit	$29.95	_____
_____	Healing Images Note Cards	$12.00	_____
_____	Ready...Set...R.E.L.A.X.	$23.95	_____
_____	Ready, Set, Release tape/CD	$10.95/15.95	_____
_____	Relaxation & Success Imagery	$10.95	_____

MUSIC SELECTIONS

		Tape / CD	
_____	*Pianoscapes* (Michael Jones)	$10.95/15.95	_____
_____	*Language of Love* (Gary Lamb)	$10.95/15.95	_____
_____	*Pachelbel w/Ocean* (Liv & Let Liv)	$10.95/15.95	_____
_____	*Bach Forever by the Sea* (D. Gibson)	$10.95/15.95	_____
_____	*The Fairy Ring* (Mike Rowland)	$10.95/15.95	_____

*Add $3.50 for first item and $.50 each additional item. **SHIPPING*** _____

WI Residents add: 5.5% **Sales Tax** _____

TOTAL _____

Orders must be accompanied by check or money order made payable to Inner Coaching.
Guaranteed — return within 30 days for refund if dissatisfied.

SHIP TO:

Name: _____

Address: _____

Phone: _____

E-Mail: _____

(This information will not be released to others.)

Please use Order Form on reverse

Please use Order Form on reverse

ORDER FORM

To order any of the resources listed below fill out this form and fax purchase order to (920) 261-8801, or mail check and order form to:

Inner Coaching, 1108 Western Avenue, Watertown, WI 53094

QTY.	ITEM	PRICE	TOTAL
_____	Healing Images for Children	$24.95	_____
_____	Healing Images for Children CD	$15.95	_____
_____	Healing Images Activity Book	$12.95	_____
_____	*Special package: above 3 items*	*$47.95*	_____
_____	Healing Images Relaxation Kit	$29.95	_____
_____	Healing Images Note Cards	$12.00	_____
_____	Ready...Set...R.E.L.A.X.	$23.95	_____
_____	Ready, Set, Release tape/CD	$10.95/15.95	_____
_____	Relaxation & Success Imagery	$10.95	_____

MUSIC SELECTIONS

Tape / CD

QTY.	ITEM	PRICE	TOTAL
_____	*Pianoscapes* (Michael Jones)	$10.95/15.95	_____
_____	*Language of Love* (Gary Lamb)	$10.95/15.95	_____
_____	*Pachelbel w/Ocean* (Liv & Let Liv)	$10.95/15.95	_____
_____	*Bach Forever by the Sea* (D. Gibson)	$10.95/15.95	_____
_____	*The Fairy Ring* (Mike Rowland)	$10.95/15.95	_____

*Add $3.50 for first item and $.50 each additional item. **SHIPPING*** _____

WI Residents add: 5.5% **Sales Tax** _____

TOTAL _____

Orders must be accompanied by check or money order made payable to Inner Coaching. Guaranteed — return within 30 days for refund if dissatisfied.

SHIP TO:

Name: _____

Address: _____

Phone: _____

E-Mail: _____

(This information will not be released to others.)